# The Startup Analysis Canvas

## Second Edition

Dr. James V. Green

Publication Data
Green, James V.
The startup analysis canvas / James V. Green
Second edition
1. Entrepreneur.  2. Innovation.

ISBN-13: 978-1720307402
ISBN-10: 1720307407

For Jamesia, Alexandra, and Vivian.

Thank you for being a part of our startup family.

# ABOUT THE AUTHOR

An award-winning educator and entrepreneur, Dr. James V. Green leads the education activities of the Maryland Technology Enterprise Institute (Mtech) at the University of Maryland. As its Director of Entrepreneurship Education, he leads nearly 30 undergraduate and graduate courses in entrepreneurship, innovation, and technology commercialization. He has created and led a host of innovative programs and activities that serve over 800,000 entrepreneurs and innovators from over 175 countries. With more than 20 publications to his credit, he is a thought leader in entrepreneurship education.

In 2011, he earned first prize in the 3E Learning Innovative Entrepreneurship Education Competition presented at the United States Association for Small Business and Entrepreneurship (USASBE). In 2013, he launched the University of Maryland's first MOOC with Coursera's "Developing Innovative Ideas for New Companies".

Prior to joining the University of Maryland, Dr. Green held founder, executive, and operational roles with multiple startups, including WaveCrest Laboratories (an innovator in next-generation electric and hybrid-electric propulsion and drive systems, acquired by Magna International, NYSE: MGA), Cyveillance (a software startup and world leader in cyber intelligence and intelligence-led security, acquired by QinetiQ, LSE: QQ.L), and NetMentors.Org (the first national online career development eMentoring community). Dr. Green earned a Doctor of Management and an MS in Technology Management from the University of Maryland University College, an MBA from the University of Michigan, and a BS in Industrial Engineering from the Georgia Institute of Technology.

# CONTENTS

# 1.0 INTRODUCTION

The Startup Analysis Canvas was created to guide first-time entrepreneurs that feel:

**Overwhelmed** by the tasks of creating a startup company,

**Frustrated** with finding the right team at the right time, and

**Disappointed** by the widespread failure of bringing good ideas to market.

It's common for aspiring entrepreneurs to desire:

**Innovation** in the approaches and tools to help create a startup company,

**Intelligence** on what customers really want, and are willing to pay for, and

**Insights** on the big picture of crafting a startup company, and the ways in which the puzzle pieces fit together.

The Startup Analysis Canvas will help you:

**Understand** the theory and practice of value creation,

**Determine** how to build the right team for your startup company,

**Avoid** wasting time with startup ideas with limited commercial potential, and

**Raise** the right financial capital at the right time for the right purpose.

By the end of this book, you will be positioned to:

**Design value propositions** that directly align with your target customers' interests,

**Assemble and lead a well-constructed team** to produce results that create value for your customers,

**Pursue big ideas** that really matter to customers, and

**Craft a financial model** that minimizes risks and maximizes your success.

The Startup Analysis Canvas provides a model for you to create your **value proposition**, **team strategy**, **market strategy**, and **financial strategy**. It is the tool at the center of this book and concretizes the process of building a startup by making the process visible and tangible through modelling; this will, in turn, make the startup process more concrete and easier to visualize, thus making the startup easier to design and manage. It perfectly integrates with The Opportunity Analysis Canvas, the precursor to this book. Together, they shape the foundation of a suite of startup creation tools.

**The Startup Analysis Canvas**

| **1** Value Proposition | | **2** Team Strategy | |
|---|---|---|---|
| | Problem | | Founders |
| | Competition | | Advisers |
| | Product-Market Fit | | Partners |

| **3** Market Strategy | | **4** Financial Strategy | |
|---|---|---|---|
| | Price | | Revenue Model |
| | Placement | | Cost Model |
| | | | Sales Model |
| | Promotion | | Funding Model |

The Opportunity Analysis Canvas is an earlier companion to The Startup Analysis Canvas.

Prior to developing the Startup Analysis Canvas is 2017, I created the Opportunity Analysis Canvas in 2013. The basic idea of the Opportunity Analysis Canvas is that before drafting business models and writing business plans, aspiring entrepreneurs need to see and think differently about problems and solutions.

As I explored this topic of entrepreneurial opportunity analysis, I recognized a pattern that could be identified. Once I identified this pattern and understood it, I saw that it was a process that could be taught.

Before writing the Opportunity Analysis Canvas book, I tested various ideas and approaches for teaching opportunity analysis over many years at the University of Maryland. These activities engaged thousands of my students in readings, assignments, projects, and mentoring that led to dramatic improvements in their entrepreneurial opportunity identification and analysis skills.

The outcome of this opportunity analysis journey and the conclusion that it could be taught successfully led to the Opportunity Analysis Canvas. It is my hope that by understanding the principles and patterns of the Opportunity Analysis Canvas, persons interested in starting a business can become more effective in identifying and analyzing entrepreneurial opportunities and realizing their personal and professional goals.

However, every journey begins with one step. Without the idea for the product or service, neither business model, nor customer discovery can begin. It is this first step of defining the idea that the Opportunity Analysis Canvas aims to help people to undertake.

The Opportunity Analysis Canvas is a tool for identifying and analyzing entrepreneurial ideas. Structured as a nine-step process, the Canvas is divided into the following parts: *thinking entrepreneurially* with an entrepreneurial mindset, entrepreneurial motivation, entrepreneurial behavior; *seeing entrepreneurially* with industry condition, industry status, macroeconomic change, and competition; and *acting entrepreneurially* with value innovation and opportunity identification.

## The Opportunity Analysis Canvas

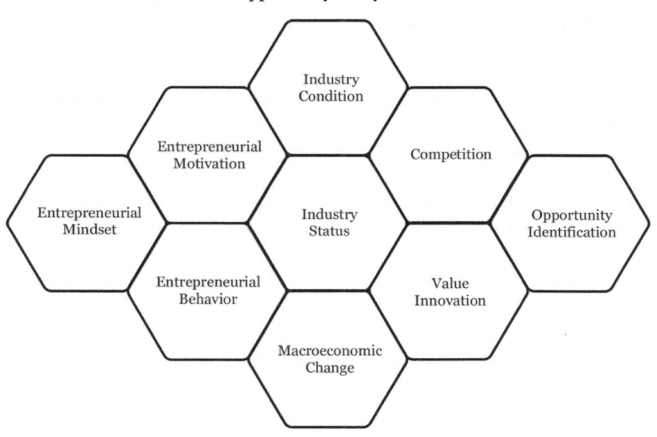

To learn more, visit www.opportunityanalysiscanvas.com.

# 1.1 HOW TO BUILD A STARTUP

Ideas on how to build a startup have evolved over time.

Ideas and models for teaching students about entrepreneurship have been emerging from universities since the 1940s. Major approaches include the following:

1. The Business Plan (1947)
2. Crossing the Chasm (1991)
3. The Innovator's Dilemma (1997)
4. The Lean Startup (2008)
5. The Business Model Canvas (2010)

The changes in the models used to teach entrepreneurship reflect changes in the requirements to launch a startup at a particular moment in time. The popular startup accelerator program, 500 Startups makes a Dinosaurs versus Cockroaches analogy when examining how the process of starting a company has changed from the 1990s to today.

In the 1990s, startups were "Big Fat Dinosaurs" that typically required complicated and expensive equipment and processes including:

- A product development cycle of twelve to twenty-four months
- A sales cycle of six to eighteen months
- Sun Servers
- Oracle Databases
- Exodus Hosting
- Raising an initial round of at least $5 million from venture capitalists

Today, startups are often "Lean Little Cockroaches" that are simpler, cheaper, and faster due to agile methodologies and inexpensive infrastructure including:

- A lean product development cycle of several days to several weeks
- Cheap rentable infrastructure and services like Amazon Web Services (AWS), Google Ads and services, PayPal and Stripe, and social media marketing
- Cloud and open source software
- Affordable, scalable sales models with online sales / Software as a Service (SaaS)
- Raising $20,000 to $100,000 in an incubator or accelerator program
- Raising a subsequent round of $1 million to $3 million from an angel group or venture capitalists

The first priority of today's startups is to demonstrate evidence of customers for the product or service before raising significant financial capital.

To illustrate this path of demonstrating evidence of a real customer, the accelerator program, 500 Startups advises startups to align their goals and activities with this path to reduce risk by securing early customers.

## The Path to Startup Risk Reduction

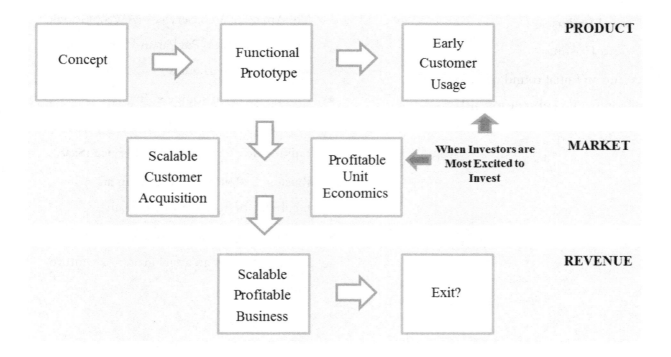

Today's startups can be

**Led** by one to three co-founders and comprised of three roles:

- Hacker: Engineers and developers to build functional prototypes (MVP)
- Hipster: Designers and user experience (UX) experts to improve UX and conversion
- Hustler: Marketing and business leads for growth hacking, scaling customer acquisition, and distributing

**Housed** in an incubator environment like 500 Startups, TechStars, or Y-Combinator or in a co-working space like WeWork

**Engaged** with active mentors and advisors through a wide variety of community-based activities

**Connected** with multiple startup peers through face-to-face and online networking platforms

The strategy for creating and launching a startup can often be accomplished with these goals:

1. Move from Prototype to Alpha in three to six months
2. Develop the Minimal Critical Feature Set
3. Get to "It Works! Someone Uses It."
4. Improve Design and Usability
5. Setup Conversion Metrics
6. Small-Scale Customer Adoption
7. Secure 10 to 1,000 users

The Startup Analysis Canvas is designed to help today's new "cockroach" startups. They operate by a different set of rules than startups of years past and live in a different business and technology ecosystem.

It all starts with the opportunity.

Startups start with an opportunity: an opportunity to solve a problem, an opportunity to be better than the status quo, an opportunity to bring a solution to the market that customers will embrace.

Casson defines entrepreneurial opportunities as "those situations in which new goods, services, raw materials, and organizing methods can be introduced and sold at greater than their cost of production."[1]

Drucker classifies entrepreneurial opportunities into three categories: "(1) the creation of new information, as occurs in the invention of new technologies; (2) the exploitations of market inefficiencies that result from information asymmetry, as occurs across time and geography; and (3) the reaction to shifts in the relative costs and benefits of alternative uses for resources, as occurs with political, regulatory, or demographic changes."[2]

By all definitions, entrepreneurial opportunities differ from the larger set of general business opportunities. Entrepreneurial opportunities require the discovery of new relationships and interactions in the marketplace that are uncertain and dynamic.

The Startup Analysis Canvas begins with defining the value proposition, the problems in the market, and your solution's ability to solve those problems. If you have an entrepreneurial idea today, you are ready to proceed with the Startup Analysis Canvas. If you are struggling to find an entrepreneurial idea that can be the basis for your startup, consider the Opportunity Analysis Canvas as a tool to identify an idea.

---

[1] Casson, M. (1982). The Entrepreneur. Totowa, NJ, US: Barnes and Noble Books.
[2] Drucker, P.F. (1985). Innovation and Entrepreneurship. New York: Harper & Row.

# 1.2 THE STARTUP ANALYSIS CANVAS

The Startup Analysis Canvas is comprised of thirteen discrete steps that are grouped into four categories. Each of these thirteen steps should be undertaken in order with the understanding that in each step, you will learn things that will prompt you to revise the work that you have done in earlier steps. The following four categories present an analysis agenda of how the thirteen steps will help you create a sustainable, innovation-based startup: value proposition, team strategy, market strategy, and financial strategy.

## The Startup Analysis Canvas

| 1 Value Proposition | | 2 Team Strategy | |
|---|---|---|---|
| | Problem | | Founders |
| | Competition | | Advisers |
| | Product-Market Fit | | Partners |

| 3 Market Strategy | | 4 Financial Strategy | |
|---|---|---|---|
| | Price | | Revenue Model |
| | Placement | | Cost Model |
| | | | Sales Model |
| | Promotion | | Funding Model |

Each of these thirteen steps are explored in their own chapters in this book, with dedicated chapters on the problem, competition, product-market fit, founders, advisers, partners, price, placement, promotion, revenue model, cost model, sales model, and funding model.

# 2.0 VALUE PROPOSITION

## So you have a great idea?

Who cares?
Why do they care?
Will they pay for it?

These are the fundamental questions for defining the value proposition, the first step in the Startup Analysis Canvas.

## What is a value proposition?

**A value proposition describes the benefits customers can expect from your product or service.**

Your value proposition is the primary reason a prospective customer will use your product or service.

Many startups mistakenly fail to define their value propositions before they launch their products or services. This failure occurs because entrepreneurs often give too much credence to their ideas, instead of understanding how these ideas would actually serve customers.

You must understand and validate the set of customer needs and wants. Instead of assuming that these needs or wants are real, it's important to validate that these needs and wants do indeed exist.

Within the Startup Analysis Canvas, the value proposition is the first category to analyze, and this analysis will include consideration of the problem, competition, and product-market fit.

There are three key purposes of a value proposition that we examine in the Startup Analysis Canvas:

- To explain how your product solves customers' problems or improves their situations
  - This addresses the Relevancy of your solution.
- To define the specific benefits that your product or service will deliver to the customer
  - This is the Quantified Value of your solution.
- To inform target customers why they should buy your product or service instead of the competition's
  - This is the Unique Differentiation of your solution.

## The Startup Analysis Canvas - Focus on Value Proposition

| 1 Value Proposition | Problem | 2 Team Strategy | Founders |
| --- | --- | --- | --- |
| | Competition | | Advisers |
| | Product-Market Fit | | Partners |

| 3 Market Strategy | Price | 4 Financial Strategy | Revenue Model |
| --- | --- | --- | --- |
| | Placement | | Cost Model |
| | | | Sales Model |
| | Promotion | | Funding Model |

To see how leading technology-based companies are communicating their value propositions to customers, consider the website for Slack, a popular communications platform.

**Slack's Value Proposition**

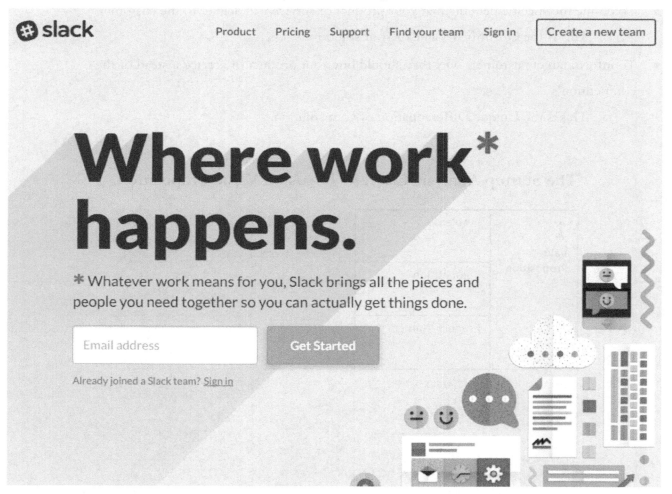

With the slogan "Where work happens," Slack informs us that it "brings all the pieces and people you need together so you can actually get things done." Without discussing their specific product features or the underlying technology, Slack communicates why their product is valuable for their target market.

# What are the typical elements of the value proposition?

The value proposition that you develop for your product or service may encompass one or more of these typical elements:

> Newness – Performance – Customization – Price – Cost Reduction –
> Design – Brand – Convenience – Accessibility

**Newness** usually influences technology-intensive products. The market for cellphones was initially very small, but once the technology became mainstream and affordable, the product became ubiquitous.

**Performance** has been a hallmark of many product offerings for decades, with most industries surviving due to improved versions of the same products. Intel doubled the speed of its chip every year, resulting in faster computers.

**Customization** supports the modern consumer's interest in self-expression and individualism. Consumers expect products that they use to be an extension of their personalities and a medium through which they can communicate their values and priorities to the world. The option to tailor the product to the consumer's preferences adds value for the customer. While customization has traditionally resulted in prohibitively expensive products, today this option provides the opportunity for customers to put their personal stamps on products more affordably.

Nike lets its customers customize their shoes through NikeID on their website. Consumers can go online and create completely original designs with their preferred color palettes and preferred placement, color, and size of the swooshes for their shoes. The customer can see what the end product will look like visually, try different permutations until the result suits h tastes, and then order the final product.

**Price** is one of the most common value proposition elements. There are many companies that enter into the market with the premise that they are providing a product or service which is cheaper than their competitors. However, organizations competing on price or offering free services may have complex business models to sustain the organization and generate revenues through other channels. Walmart and Southwest Airlines are two longtime, high-performing companies with low price as a core value proposition.

**Design** is, historically speaking, important for clothing labels that demand higher prices because of the superior design. Prada can charge hundreds of dollars for a t-shirt because of the strength of its design and brand. The value of design is increasingly extending into consumer electronics and many other product lines.

**Cost Reduction** focuses on reducing the initial and/or ongoing cost that a customer pays for owning and/or operating a product or service. Technology has played a great role in helping consumers reduce costs. One such example is Salesforce.com which allows customers to use a customer relationship management software for a fee, voiding the need for the customer to buy the software, hardware and install and run it, each action associated with a significant cost.

**Brand** can be clustered with Design because the appeal is quite similar. Customers may show loyalty to a brand because of its design or because of the perceived status the brand name itself lends to the owner or user. While a Rolex is a watch, it is a statement that the wearer has money and status. Ultimately, a brand-intensive product aims to help the customer look and feel in control, important, and part of a desirable group.

**Convenience** is characterized by ease of use. One example of this type of value proposition is Apple's iconic iPod, which provided consumers with a convenient way to listen to music. By pairing it with iTunes, Apple increased the convenience of finding and listening to music significantly; enabling users to search for, download, and play songs easily.

**Accessibility** makes a previously inaccessible product or service available to a consumer segment. Innovative technologies and variations in business models have both led to improving accessibility for serviced customers. NetJets is an example of a company which provides accessibility to transportation. The company allows individuals and corporations to have access to private jets, access which has traditionally been cost prohibitive and therefore unavailable to many who did not have the money to afford this luxury.

## What makes a winning value proposition?

In the process of creating a value proposition, remember that it's for real people to read and understand. Here's an example of an ineffective value proposition:

**"Revenue-focused marketing automation and sales effectiveness solutions to unleash collaboration throughout the revenue generation ecosystem"**

Your value proposition should be clear and concise, using language that your target customers understand. The value proposition should fit within your customer's conceptual framework. In order to accomplish this, you need to understand your target customers and how they may benefit from your product or service.

**Be clear.**

It's brief and easy to understand. Avoid hype (like "never seen before amazing miracle product"), superlatives ("best") and business jargon ("value-added interactions"). Communicate the benefits (in other words, the value). Show what's different or better about your product or service than that of your competitors. The best value proposition is clear.

**Be succinct.**

If potential customers have to read a lot of text to understand what you are offering, you're doing it wrong. Sufficient information is crucial for conversions, but you need to draw them in with a clear, compelling value proposition first.

Be clear and succinct when explaining:

- Who the product or service is for,
- What product or service your company is selling,
- What the benefits of using it are, and
- What makes your product or service unique when compared to that of the competitors.

To develop your answers to these and other questions, conduct market research and competitive analysis via databases, online searches because it is a helpful first step to help you to understand your target customers and competitors. To fully develop your understanding, you will need answers that are directly voiced by your target customer and specific to your product or service. You will have to interview your target customers to truly understand them and to best assess the potential success of your startup.

Evernote's winning value proposition is promoted on the homepage of their website:

**Evernote's Value Proposition**

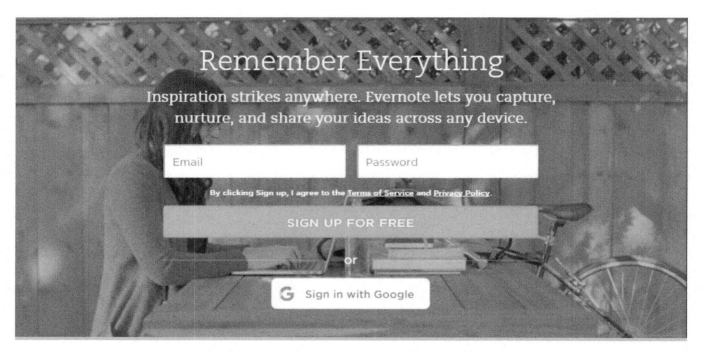

By enabling customers to "remember everything," Evernote recognizes that "inspiration strikes everywhere." Further, Evernote "lets you capture, nurture, and share your ideas across any device."

Evernote's value proposition aligns with the pains and gains that their target customers experience.

| PRODUCTS AND SERVICES | PAIN RELIEVERS | GAIN CREATORS |
|---|---|---|
| • One workspace for all<br>• Write every day<br>• Work together<br>• Gather research<br>• Find everything fast<br>• Share your ideas<br>• Stay in sync | • Removes the need to carry notebooks, consolidated notes, or other forms of data around<br>• Removes the need for complicated slides during meetings<br>• Provides a single place to save online material available on a topic of interest<br>• Is economically accessible for individuals, all without requiring a heavy investment in hardware or software | • Provides a common working space for a team to share ideas and information<br>• Provides freelancers and other users access to a free service in which his or her notes are backed up and available to him or her at a moment's notice,<br>• Cost effective for individuals who can use the service for free<br>• Provides tools that help customers effectively and efficiently plan and execute pro |

# What are the steps to creating the value proposition?

To develop your value proposition, follow these four steps:

1. **Define the problem to determine whether it's a problem worth solving.** Inventor Charles Kettering said, "a problem well stated is a problem half solved." Many aspiring entrepreneurs make the mistake of diving into their solutions before really understanding the problem or need facing the target customer.

2. **Evaluate whether your solution solves the problem uniquely.** After you've validated the problem with target customers, ask yourself what is unique about your solution. A useful approach is to think of your solution in the context of the 3Ds: What unique combination of (D)iscontinuous innovation, (D)efensible technology, and (D)isruptive business model are you bringing to the market?

3. **Measure the potential for customer adoption.** Most aspiring entrepreneurs are overly focused on the features of that product and pay insufficient attention to how hard it will be for customers to learn to use their products. The Gain/Pain ratio involves measuring the gain you deliver the customer versus the pain and cost the customer will face when adopting and adapting to your product. Ideally, you should deliver non-disruptive solutions (i.e., solutions that offer substantial benefits with minimal cost and little effort for the target customer). In other words, seek a disruptive innovation that is non-disruptive for customers to purchase and use.

4. **Craft the value proposition.** Once you have completed the defining, evaluating, and measuring steps, you are ready to craft your value proposition. This framework is useful for creating your value proposition in a clear, concise manner that is inclusive of the key criteria of a winning value proposition.

Create your own value proposition by filling in the (phrases) in this framework.

**For (target customers)**

**Who are dissatisfied with (the current alternative),**

**Our product is a (new product)**

**That provides (key problem-solving capability)**

**Unlike (the product alternative).**

Also, do not lose sight of the fact that you are core to your startup's value proposition. Consider these questions as you are developing the value proposition:

**What problems do you understand uniquely well?**

**What solution can you deliver uniquely well?**

**What kind of disruptive business model can you bring to the market based on your insights and capabilities?**

The value proposition framework is visible in Quicken's home page for their website. "From budgeting for your summer vacation to planning for the future, we make managing your money a snap."

## Quicken's Value Proposition

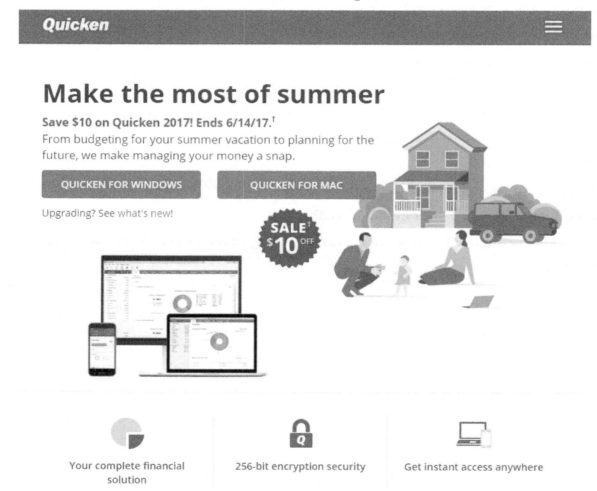

# 2.1 PROBLEM

A significant part of defining a value proposition involves understanding the problem experienced by your target customers. If you find yourself answering a definitive yes to the majority of these questions, then you are on the right path toward building a compelling value proposition. If not, consider re-evaluating and revising your startup idea. Consider the 4Us of Problem Definition to get started:

- **Is the problem Urgent?** Is it one of the top few priorities for your target customer? Particularly if the end-user of your product or service is a business (i.e., you're selling social media marketing software to coffee shops), it's difficult to capture their attention and resources unless the problem that you can solve is urgent.

- **Is the problem Underserved?** Is there an absence of viable solutions to the problem that you aim to solve? Focus on the white space, or empty space, in the market. As a startup, your likelihood of success is higher if you are bringing a new type of solution to the market instead of competing head-to-head with established competitors.

- **Is the problem Unworkable?** Does your solution fix a broken situation or process in which there are real, measurable consequences to inaction? If you are selling to businesses, will someone be fired if the issue is not addressed? If the answer is yes, then that person will likely be your internal champion.

- **Is fixing the problem Unavoidable?** Is the problem driven by a mandate, one with implications associated with governance or regulatory control? For example, is it driven by a fundamental requirement for accounting, compliance, or privacy?

While your solution may not earn the highest marks for all of the 4Us, you will benefit from addressing at least one, and preferably several, of them.

# Is the problem conspicuous and critical?

In addition to applying the 4Us framework to analyze the problem, further questions can qualify the problem. Is it conspicuous or concealed? Is it a craving or critical? Does it address a white space in the market, allowing you to capitalize on an open area of opportunity?

In business to business (B2B) markets, you want to be in the position of addressing problems that are conspicuous and critical, as they are far more acute than those that are concealed and a craving. Conspicuous and critical problems stand in the way of business. They put careers and reputations at risk. Concealed problems are unacknowledged, and this means they often require costly missionary selling. Craving problems are optional and as such, are the hardest of products for a B2B startup to sell.

While conspicuous and critical problems also contribute to success with business to consumer (B2C) products, there are a number of success stories in B2C that are based on exposing latent craving needs. Facebook is a great example. When examining B2C customers, consider consumer needs through frameworks like Maslow's hierarchy of needs, a model which states that humans will meet more urgent needs first (survival needs) before meeting less urgent needs. Facebook, because it satisfied our obvious social needs, was able to capitalize on meeting those needs and was thus financially successful.

Or consider Evernote and its value proposition. The company set out to "help the world remember everything, communicate effectively, and get things done". From saving thoughts and ideas to preserving experiences to working efficiently with others, Evernote's unique collection of apps makes it easy for users to stay organized and be productive.

Rover, a dog care provider app and website, provides a solution for dog walking, dog boarding, and a variety of related services. While their solution may not be valuable to everyone, there is a sizeable target market for which they offer tremendous value.

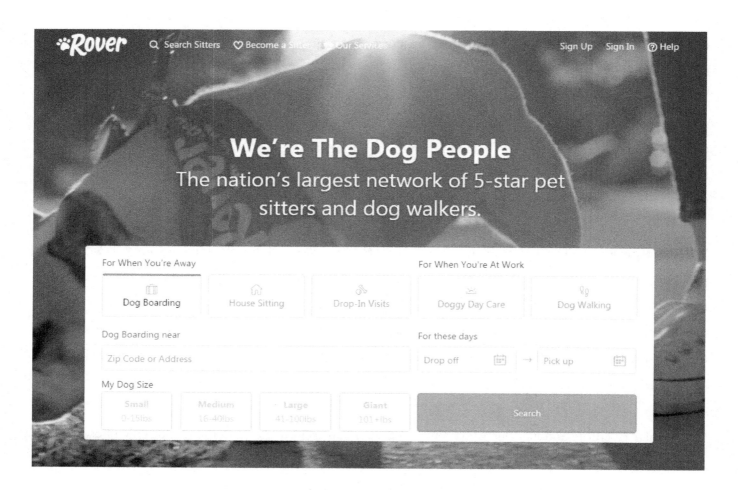

The value proposition that Rover's solution delivers is evidenced in their ability to generate revenue and raise financial capital for their startup at a valuation of nearly $300 million in 2016.

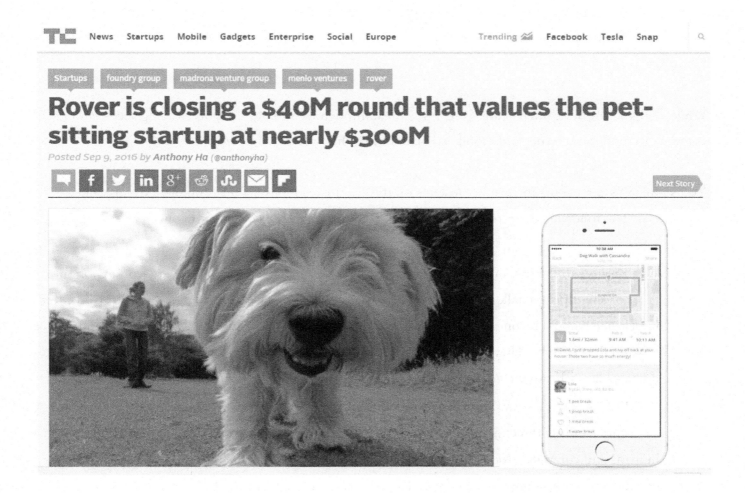

# What problems excite startup accelerators?

In September 2016, startup accelerator Y Combinator's "Requests for Startups" shared startup ideas they've been waiting for people to propose. In an effort to be more direct, they're introducing RFSs (Requests for Startups).

While a number of these interest areas are in the breakthrough technology category, leading accelerators will continue to fund the Internet and mobile companies that they've funded in the past.

You shouldn't start a company just because it's on this list. Instead, this list may stimulate you to think about ideas. The following descriptions are sourced from http://www.ycombinator.com/rfs/

- A.I.: Relative to the potential impact, it doesn't seem like enough smart people are working on this. A lot of smart people talk about AI with a combination of awe and fear, both for good reasons. But it feels like it could be one of the dividing lines in the history of technology, where before and after look totally different. They're especially interested in people applying new research to "narrow" domains like self-driving cars, drug discovery, programming assistance, and fraud detection.
- BIOTECH: It's still early, but it seems like we are finally making real progress hacking biology. There are so many directions this new field can take: fighting disease, slowing aging, merging humans and computers, downloading memories, genetic programming, among others. We are certain that this is going to be a surprising, powerful, and controversial field over the next several decades. It is certainly a burgeoning new field with lots of possibilities; in fact, the environment surrounding this feels is similar to the one surrounding microcomputers in the 1970s. For example, reading DNA has become incredibly fast and cheap, and there are many interesting applications for

the technology. There will perhaps be even more interesting applications as we get better at writing DNA. We are especially interested in applications of biotech to prevent its misuses. For example, if the bad guys can create new infectious diseases quickly, it'd be nice if the good guys could create new cures and vaccines quickly as well.

- COMPUTER SECURITY: Securing computers is difficult because the work required is so asymmetric – the attacker only has to find one flaw, while a defender has to protect against every possible weakness. Unfortunately, securing computers isn't just hard, it's critically and increasingly important. As the software revolution continues and more critical information and systems are connected to the Internet, we become more vulnerable to cyberattacks, and the disruptions those attacks cause are more severe.

- DIVERSITY: A diverse workforce is good for business and good for the world. Without different perspectives, the products and services we create will miss big opportunities to provide solutions to large segments of people. We want to fund non-profits and startups that are working on making technology a place that is more inclusive and attractive to people of all ages, races, sexual orientations, and cultures.

- EDUCATION: If we can fix education, we can eventually do everything else on this list. The first attempts to use technology to fix education have focused on using the Internet to distribute traditional content to a wider audience. This is good, but the Internet is a fundamentally different medium and capable of much more. Solutions that combine the mass scale of technology with one-on-one, in-person interaction are particularly intriguing and could be implemented more and then evaluated in terms of their educational impact.

- ENERGY: There is a remarkable correlation between the cost of energy and quality of life. Throughout history, when the cost of energy has come down a lot (for example, with the steam engine) quality of life has drastically improved. Cheap energy would do quite a lot to reduce poverty.

New energy sources could also help the environment, improve the economy, reduce war, ensure a stable future, make food and water more abundant, and much more. We believe economics will dominate—new sources of energy must be cheaper than old ones without the need for subsidies and be able to scale to meet global demand. Nuclear energy might meet the mark and also possibly renewables. But pricing is the first order question. In addition to energy generation, we're also interested in energy storage and transmission. Batteries that can store ten times more energy would enable important new technologies, as would the ability to easily move energy around.

- ENTERPRISE SOFTWARE: Software used by large companies is still not of sufficient quality or utility, yet it is still very lucrative. Category-defining enterprise software companies will emerge to solve problems for every vertical, every business size, and every job function. Here are three specific areas we think are particularly interesting:
  - Making The Expensive Cheap: Because of the cost of traditional enterprise software, many categories of solutions were previously too cost prohibitive to be of benefit to small or even medium-sized businesses.
  - The Next Billion Workers: Traditionally, office-based knowledge workers have been the users of enterprise software. Mobile phones and tablets turn every type of employee—from the retail store associate to the field services team—into a knowledge worker.
  - Digitizing Every Industry: Every industry is going through some form of information-based disruption; this is causing businesses to modernize their practices by leveraging new data, accelerating key processes, and delivering digitally-enabled experiences in the process.

- FINANCIAL SERVICES: The world's financial systems are increasingly unable to meet the demands of consumers and businesses. That fact makes some sense because regulations designed to protect customers can't change fast enough to keep up with the pace at which technology is changing the needs of those customers. This mismatch creates inefficiencies at almost every level of the financial system. These inefficiencies have an impact on how people invest their savings, how businesses gain access to capital to grow, how risk is priced and insured, and how financial firms do business with each other. We think that software will accelerate the pace at which financial services change and will eventually shift the nature of regulations. We want to fund companies with novel ideas of how to make that happen.

- FOOD AND FARMING: An estimated forty percent of the world's workforce works in agriculture. Better food and farming techniques that provide more and better food could increase the world's health, unlock the potential of numerous workers, and improve living conditions for billions of animals. We believe economics will dominate—reducing cost while preserving or improving flavor will win the day.

- FUTURE OF WORK: Jobs will look very different twenty-five years from now. We've already seen a massive shift toward automation, and the pace of technology's impact on work isn't slowing down. A study by the World Economic Forum estimates that in the next five years, five million jobs in fifteen economies will be lost. They're interested in what comes next. People seek full-time jobs for many reasons, including money, healthcare, and a sense of purpose. We'd love to see solutions that address each of these factors (or any others) in anticipation of a changing job market.

- GLOBAL HEALTH NON-PROFITS: There are lots of cheap, proven ways to save and improve people's lives. They should be reaching everyone. Why do so many people in the developing world still suffer for lack of simple things like bednets, vaccines, and iodized salt? Part of the problem is money, and they're interested in new ways to get people to give. Part of it is execution, and we'd love to see nonprofits that are truly data literate and metrics driven closing these gaps. Organizations like GiveWell have large amounts of funding at the ready for provably effective global health interventions.

- HEALTHCARE: Healthcare in the United States is badly broken. We are getting close to spending twenty percent of our GDP on healthcare; this is unsustainable. They're interested in ways to make healthcare better for less money, not in companies that are able to exploit the system by overcharging. They're especially interested in preventative healthcare, as this is probably the means of improve health with the highest leverage. Sensors and data are interesting in lots of different areas, but especially for healthcare. Medical devices also seem like fertile ground for startups.

- HOLLYWOOD 2.0: New celebrities aren't discovered by talent agents; they are discovered directly by their fans on YouTube. In 2014, movies had their worst summer since 1997. Just like future celebrities are unlikely to get their start with talent agencies, future content consumers will watch content online instead of at the theater and probably in very different ways. Celebrities now have direct relationships with their fans through media such as Twitter. Members of the entertainment industry can also distribute content in new ways. There are almost certainly huge new businesses that will get built as part of this shift.

- HUMAN AUGMENTATION: They like companies that try to augment humans. This is a general category because there are a lot of different ways to do this. Biotech can help us live longer and be smarter. Robots can help us accomplish physical tasks we otherwise couldn't. Software can help us focus on simple actions that make us happier and help large groups of us organize ourselves better.

- IMPROVING DEMOCRACY: There are thousands of ways technology can be applied to improve democracy. For democracy to function effectively, more of us need to be engaged and empowered. We'd like to see startups and non-profits who are using technology to make it easier and more appealing to get involved in the political process. We want technology that makes it easy to understand how new laws and programs impact citizens, programs that teach people how to run for office, and communication tools that make it easier for citizens to be heard by their representatives. We'd like to see tools that address problems in the voting process, problems such as voter suppression and gerrymandering.

- MASS MEDIA: What can we do to bring up the baseline and make the vast majority of our mass media better? Media outlets that rely on polarization, misinformation, passivity, and fear are not improving society. They're looking for ways to get the media to produce more quality programming and thus improve mass media.

- NEWS: We need an accurate, unbiased press for our democracy to work. They're facing two major issues with news. The first is fake news. The business model for online media rewards the people who get the greatest number of page views, clicks, and likes. That results in a system that prizes virality over truth. Building tools for fact-checking sources will become increasingly important. Second is the issue of protecting the freedom of the press. They're looking to fund tools that can help protect and defend journalists and their sources.

- ONE MILLION JOBS: They want to fund companies that have the potential to create a million jobs. There are a lot of areas where it makes sense to divide labor between humans and computers—we are very good at some things computers are terrible at and vice versa—and some of these require a huge amount of human resources. This is both good for the world and likely a good business strategy—as existing jobs go away, a company that creates a lot of new jobs should be able to get a lot of talented people.

- PHARMACEUTICALS: Drug development has become slower and more expensive. They'd like to fund companies doing pharmaceutical research in new ways. They're interested in substances that may not become prescription drugs, but still really help people. Areas like nootropics seem underexplored.

- PROGRAMMING TOOLS: Software developers are shaping a bigger and bigger portion of our daily lives. The products used to make software are a powerful lever: these products have a dramatic impact on the quality and kind of software being built. They're interested in helping developers create better software, faster. This includes new ways to write, understand, and collaborate on code, as well as the next generation of tools and infrastructure for delivering software continuously and reliably. They believe it's especially important to build products that make software development accessible to the largest part of our society. In fact, they're especially interested in new ways to program. There are probably much better ways for people to program, and figuring one out would have a huge impact on the world of computing. Up to now, the improvements have been incremental: he frameworks are better, and the languages a bit more clever; however, for the most part these changes are small upgrades in old methods. One way to think about this is to consider what might come after programming languages.

- ROBOTICS: Robots will be a major means of getting tasks accomplishments in the physical world. Our definition of what constitutes a robot is pretty broad: for example, we count a self-driving car as a robot. Robots are how we'll likely explore space and maybe even the human body.

- TRANSPORTATION & HOUSING: About half of all energy is used on transportation, and people spend a great amount of time unhappily commuting. Face-to-face interaction is still really important; therefore, people still need to move around. Also, housing continues to become more expensive, partially due to difficulties in transportation. They're interested in better ways for people to live somewhere nice and still work together, through improvement in home-to-work and back commutes. Specifically, lightweight, short-distance personal transportation is a topic of great interest.

- UNDERSERVED COMMUNITIES AND SOCIAL SERVICES: Tens of millions of working poor in America don't see a path to the middle class. This population has to navigate a world with substandard services, low quality housing, overcrowded schools, and crime in their neighborhoods. Often they don't have a bank account and live paycheck to paycheck. The US government alone spends hundreds of billions of dollars per year on social services and safety net programs for these underserved communities. They believe great non-profits and for-profits can bring technology and strong metrics-driven approaches to this largely ignored, massive market.

- VR AND AR: Virtual reality and augmented reality have been a long-unfulfilled promise. But we feel the wave is coming, and this is the right time to start working on it.

- WATER: Global water demand will increase fifty percent by 2050. The world is close to a tipping point in which technology will let us make clean water extremely abundant and cheap. We will create more than enough clean water for everyone in the world, for any use necessary.

# Is the problem worth solving?

The aim of asking the question, "Is the problem worth solving?," is to discern whether or not there are enough customers willing to pay you to solve their problem(s). Customers may pay you directly, or they may participate in the business model that you've developed to monetize your idea. In this context, the unit of measure for "worth" is money. While there are many problems that are worthy of being solved in society, the focus of our attention will be those problems that can be solved with a feasible economic model that is not reliant on donations, corporate charity, government grants, and related philanthropic funding. We will focus on building startups that can be self-sufficient after startup funding is secured.

Once the existence of the problem has been assessed with the questions of Urgency, Undeservedness, Unworkability, and Unavoidabilty, determining if the problem is worth solving requires answering further questions.

### Who is your customer?

This is the first step to defining your market and understanding their needs and wants. Analysis of industries, markets, and value innovations narrows the focus to real customers.

### What are their needs & wants?

Focus on customer value first. Why do they need your product or service? What benefits will they gain? Can they make money or save money with your product? Can they save time with your product? Are there any other benefits for them?

### Are there enough customers?

If you have a real customer and if you can deliver real value, then ask yourself how many people experience these problems now? In the future? How many buyers are there? Are there enough people who care about this problem for you to be financially successful by solving the problem?

It's never too early to talk to prospective customers.

It is highly valuable to validate your ideas about the problem by talking with prospective customers very early in the startup process. You should engage with customers pre-prototype to get their insights on what features and values matter to them. Only by knowing your customers and understanding what they are willing to pay for the product that you envision can you consider if the time and money required to develop the product is worth it. These insights are critical to understand the market's size and its potential.

To effectively answer the question of whether the problem is worth solving, you also need to understand the specifics of the target customers who experience the problem. This is your target customer segment.

Customer segments are the community of customers or businesses that you are aiming to sell your product or services to. Customer segments are one of the most important building blocks of the Startup Analysis Canvas for your business, so getting these insights right is key to your success.

Customers can be segmented into distinct groups based on needs, behaviors, and other traits that they share. A customer segment may also be defined through demographics such as age, ethnicity, profession, gender or on psychographic factors such as spending behavior, interests, and motivations. You may choose to target a single group or multiple groups with your products and services.

By matching your customer segment to your value proposition, you can achieve a more lucrative revenue stream. Hence, it is fundamental for startups to understand the trade-offs between different customer segments and carefully select which segment it wants to target. Then, the startup must create a value proposition and employ a business model best suited to servicing their chosen customer segment's needs.

You can categorize consumers into distinct groups if they have the following characteristics:

- The groups have a particular need which justifies the creation of a product to match this need.

- The group needs a separate distribution channel in order to be reached.

- The groups require relationships of different kinds.

- There is a very clear difference in the level of profitability each group represents for the organization.

- Each consumer group feels strongly enough to pay for a different version of the product or service, tailored to meet their preferences.

# What is customer discovery?

Customer discovery is the process used to identify your target customer segment. The goals of customer discovery are to first validate the problem and later validate the fit of your solution to that problem. Alternatively, you may invalidate the problem and/or solution early in the startup's lifetime, saving you the time and money of pursuing a fruitless startup idea.

With customer discovery, you can begin to identify and test your first version of your product or service, called the minimum viable product (MVP). You can get insights for pattern recognition to guide you in product development, operations, marketing, etc.

Business ideas are based on assumptions that need validation. Talking to prospective customers is critical to validating that your perceived problem is real and worth solving.

Customer discovery is NOT about:

- Asking your friends and family if they like your product or service,
- Evangelizing your vision, or
- Pitching your solution.

While there's a tendency to try to sell people on your idea, your job in customer discovery is to learn from prospective customers. Friends and family may be biased in their feedback because you have an existing relationship.

You are a detective. Seek clues that help confirm or deny your assumptions about the problem. Is their interest among prospective customers in solving the problem and in using your solution?

Customer discovery is best done via face-to-face interviews or else a video conference with Zoom, Skype, or some similar Internet application. Avoid surveys and emails, as these offer little real value in really understanding customers when compared to interviews.

To prepare for your customer discovery interviews, begin with core questions, such as the following:

- Whom do you want to learn about (i.e., who do you think your customer is)?
- What do you want to learn?
- How will you get to the interview?
- How can you ensure an effective session?
- How do you make sense of what you learn?

Further questions that you should be able to answer after your interviews may include:

- Who will my target customer be?
- What problem does my customer wants to solve?
- What will solve my customer's problem?
- Why can't my customer solve this today?
- What is the measurable outcome my customer wants to achieve?
  What primary tactic will I utilize to acquire customers? Who will my earliest adopter will be? By what means will I earn money?
- Who will my primary competition be?
- How will I primarily beat my competitors?
- What is my biggest risk to financial viability?
- What is my biggest technical risk?
- What faulty assumptions would cause this business to fail?

A terrific resource on how to conduct customer discovery is Talking to Humans by Giff Constable. In this free pdf available from his website, Giff shares insights on questions such as

- Whom do you need to learn from?
- What do you need to learn from the market?
- How do you find the right people to interview?
- How can you ensure an effective session?
- How do you turn observations into decisions and actions?
- How can you avoid the most common mistakes people make?

## 2.2 COMPETITION

Every business faces competition. Understanding the strengths and weaknesses of your competition, or potential competition, is critical to making sure your business survives and grows. You should thoroughly assess your competition on a regular basis.

Startups are especially vulnerable to competition, especially when new companies enter a marketplace.

While competitive analysis can be incredibly complicated and time-consuming, it doesn't have to be. Here is a simple three-step process that you can follow to identify, analyze, and determine the strengths and weaknesses of your competition on an ongoing basis:

**Step 1: Profile current competitors**

**Step 2: Identify and profile potential competitors**

**Step 3: Develop your competitive position**

We will examine each in turn and note important questions to consider at each step.

# Step 1: Profile current competitors

First, develop a basic profile of each of your current competitors, including both online and offline competitors.

In the beginning, analyze companies that are direct competitors. If you plan to develop a financial management app, you will compete with other apps that focus on financial management.

Once you identify your direct competitors, answer these questions objectively with research and analysis. It's easy to assume weaknesses in your competition without thoughtful research to support your claims. Also, be sure to recognize and admit areas where competitors may be able to outperform you.

- **What are their strengths?**
  - Price, service, convenience, and brand are all areas where you may be vulnerable.
- **What are their weaknesses?**
  - Weaknesses are opportunities you may be able to take advantage of.
- **What are their basic objectives?**
  - Do they seek to gain market share?
  - Do they attempt to capture premium clients?
  - What are they trying to achieve?
- **What are their marketing strategies?**
  - What is evident in their advertising, public relations, and the like.?
- **How can you capture market share from them?**
- **How will they respond when you enter the market?**

To gather this information, you can

- **Analyze competitors' websites and marketing materials.**
  - o Important information that you need about their products, services, prices, and company objectives may be readily available. If that information is not available, you may have identified a weakness.

- **Visit their locations if they have an offline presence.**
  - o Collect their sales materials and promotional literature.
  - o Also, ask friends to stop in or call to ask for information.

- **Evaluate their marketing and advertising campaigns.**
  - o How a company advertises creates a great opportunity to uncover the objectives and strategies of that company.
  - o Analyzing its advertising should help you determine how a company positions itself, who it markets to, and what strategies it employs to reach potential customers.

- **Browse.**
  - o Search the Internet for news, public relations, and other discussion of your competition.
  - o Search blogs and Twitter feeds, as well as review and recommendation sites. While most of the information you find will be anecdotal and based on the opinion of just a few people, you may be able to at least get a sense of how some consumers perceive your competition. Plus, you may get advance warning about expansion plans, new markets they intend to enter, or changes in management.

# Step 2: Identify and profile potential competitors

It is difficult to predict when and where new competition might arise. To develop your insights, regularly search for news on your industry, your products, your services, and your target market.

There are other ways to predict when competition may follow you into a market. Other people may see the same business opportunity that you see. Think about your business and your industry, and if the following conditions exist, you may face competition in the future:

- The industry enjoys relatively high profit margins.
- Entering the market is relatively easy and inexpensive.
- The market is growing.
    - The more rapidly it is growing, the greater the risk of competition.
- Supply and demand is unbalanced.
    - If supply is low and demand is high, expect competitors to enter the market to serve this unmet demand.
- If minimal competition exists, there may be space for new competitors to enter the market

In summary, if serving your market seems easy, you can safely assume competitors will enter your market. A sound strategy anticipates and accounts for new competitors.

# A Brief Competitive View on Ridesharing Services

PRODUCT

STRENGTHS &
WEAKNESSES

**Strengths**

- The goals this user hopes to achieve.
- A task that needs to be completed.
- A life goal to be reached. A life goal to be reached.

**Weaknesses**

- The goals this user hopes to achieve.
- A task that needs to be completed.
- A life goal to be reached. A life goal to be reached.

**Strengths**

- The goals this user hopes to achieve.
- A task that needs to be completed.
- A life goal to be reached. A life goal to be reached.

**Weaknesses**

- The goals this user hopes to achieve.
- A task that needs to be completed.
- A life goal to be reached. A life goal to be reached.

**Strengths**

- The goals this user hopes to achieve.
- A task that needs to be completed.
- A life goal to be reached. A life goal to be reached.

**Weaknesses**

- The goals this user hopes to achieve.
- A task that needs to be completed.
- A life goal to be reached. A life goal to be reached.

MARKET
BREAKDOWN

 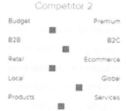 

Competitor 1

Budget    Premium
B2B    B2C
Retail    Ecommerce
Local    Global
Products    Services

Competitor 2

Budget    Premium
B2B    B2C
Retail    Ecommerce
Local    Global
Products    Services

Competitor 3

Budget    Premium
B2B    B2C
Retail    Ecommerce
Local    Global
Products    Services

# Step 3: Develop your competitive position

Once you've profiled the current and potential competitors, distill what you've learned by answering the following questions:

- **Who are my current competitors?**
  - What is their market share?
  - How successful are they?
- **Which market do current competitors target?**
  - Do they focus on a specific customer type, on serving the mass market, or on a particular niche?
- **Are competing businesses growing or scaling back their operations?**
  - Why?
  - What does that mean for your business?
- **How will your company be different from the competition?**
  - What competitor weaknesses can you exploit?
  - What competitor strengths will you need to overcome to be successful?
- **What will you do if competitors drop out of the marketplace?**
  - What will you do to take advantage of the opportunity?
- **What will you do if new competitors enter the marketplace?**
  - How will you react to and overcome new challenges?

Competitive analysis does more than help you to understand your competition. Competitive analysis can also help you to identify changes you should make to your business strategies. Learn from competitor strengths, take advantage of competitor's weaknesses, and apply the same analysis to your own startup.

# 2.3 PRODUCT-MARKET FIT

Product-market fit is one of the most important modern concepts for aspiring and active entrepreneurs. It is also one of the most misunderstood.

Marc Andreessen coined the term. He is the co-author of Mosaic, the first widely used Web browser; co-founder of Netscape; and co-founder and general partner of Silicon Valley venture capital firm, Andreessen Horowitz. He's also served as a board of director for Facebook, eBay, and Hewlett Packard.

In a 2007 blog post, Marc Andreessen stated,

**"Product-market fit means being in a good market with a product that can satisfy that market."**

While there are thousands of articles and references that mention the term, few provide detailed guidance on how to actually achieve product-market fit as a startup.

## The Product-Market Fit Pyramid

The Product-Market Fit Pyramid is a valuable guide through this process. It is an action-oriented model that defines product-market fit using five key components. In this hierarchical model, each component is a layer of the pyramid. Each layer is directly related to the levels above and below it. Starting with the bottom of the five layers of the Product-Market Fit Pyramid, your tasks are to examine your target customer, your customer's underserved needs, your value proposition, your feature set, and your user experience (UX).

**The Product-Market Fit Pyramid**

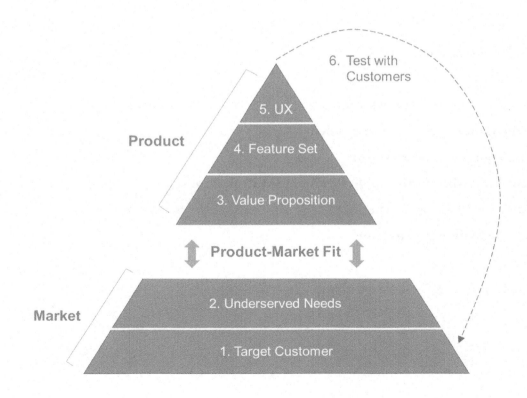

In the process of trying to define and build a successful product, you can form and test your hypotheses in all five of these areas. The Product-Market Fit Pyramid helps you to be more explicit and rigorous about these hypotheses.

## The Lean Product Process

The Lean Product Process is an iterative, easy-to-follow process based on the Product-Market Fit Pyramid. This process guides you sequentially through each layer of the pyramid from the bottom to the top. The process helps you articulate, test, and revise your key hypotheses so that you can improve your product-market fit.

The Lean Product Process consists of six steps:

1. **Determine your target customer**
2. **Identify underserved customer needs**
3. **Define your value proposition**
4. **Specify your Minimum Viable Product (MVP) feature set**
5. **Create your MVP prototype**
6. **Test your MVP with customers**

We will examine each of these six steps in turn.

## Step 1: Determine your target customer.

It all begins with targeting customers who will ultimately decide how well your product meets their needs. You should use market segmentation to focus on your target customer. Personas are a great way to describe your target customer so that you understand for whom you should be designing and building the product.

You may not have a precise vision of your target customer at the outset. That is typical. It's fine to start with a high-level hypothesis about who your target customer is and then revise it as you learn and iterate.

## Step 2: Identify underserved customer needs.

After forming your hypothesis about your target customers, the next step is to understand their needs and wants. As you try to create value for customers, you want to identify the specific needs and wants that correspond to a good market opportunity. For example, you may avoid a market where customers are extremely happy with how well the existing solutions meet their needs and wants.

When you develop a new product or improve an existing product, focus on addressing customer needs that aren't adequately met by existing competitors. These are their "underserved" needs. Customers are going to evaluate your product in relation to the alternatives. The relative degree to which your product meets their needs depends on the competitive landscape.

## Step 3: Define your value proposition.

Your value proposition is your plan for how your product will meet customer needs better than the alternatives. Of all the potential customer needs your product could address, which ones will you focus on with your product?

**"People think focus means saying yes to the thing you've got to focus on. But that's not what it means at all. It means saying no to the hundred other good ideas that there are. You have to pick carefully. I'm actually as proud of the things we haven't done as the things I have done. Innovation is saying no to one thousand things."**

**Steve Jobs**

You need to figure out how your product will be differentiated from competitive products. How will your product outperform the others? What unique features of your product will please customers? This is the essence of product strategy.

## Step 4: Specify your MVP feature set.

Once you are clear on your value proposition, you need to specify what functionalities your minimum viable product will include. You don't want to spend time and effort toiling away, only to find out later that customers don't want the product you've built. The MVP approach is aimed at building only what is needed to create enough value in the eyes of your target customer to validate that you are heading in the right direction.

Customers may end up telling you that your MVP lacks an important functionality. Or they may tell you that they wouldn't use a particular feature that you decided to include in your MVP. The goal is to iterate until you have an MVP that customers agree is viable and that aligns with a pricing strategy that makes sense for you.

## Step 5: Create your MVP prototype.

In order to test your MVP hypotheses with customers, you need to show them a version of your product so they can give you feedback on it. You will need to apply user experience (UX) design to bring your feature set to life for your customers.

While you could build a live, working version of your MVP, it's typically faster and cheaper to create an MVP prototype. A prototype is a representation of your product that you create without having to build your actual product.

Prototypes can vary in fidelity, the level of detail to which they resemble the final product, and interactivity, the degree to which the user can interact with the prototype compared to the final product. A hand sketch of your product (on paper or a whiteboard) would be low fidelity and low interactivity. For web and mobile products, medium-fidelity wireframes and high-fidelity mockups are frequently used.

You can use a set of high-fidelity mockups of your product to create an interactive prototype. Prototyping tools are useful to specify clickable links for software and apps. These simulate the user experience of the final product with enough fidelity and interactivity to obtain valuable feedback from customers.

# Fidelity versus Interactivity in the MVP

High

Interactive
Prototype
that Appears
"Real"

**Fidelity** is the level of detail
to which the prototype
resembles the final product.

Wireframe with
Functions Drawn

Hand
Drawing

Low

**Interactivity** is the degree to which the
user can interact with the prototype
compared to the final product.

# From Sketch to Wireframe to Prototype for an App

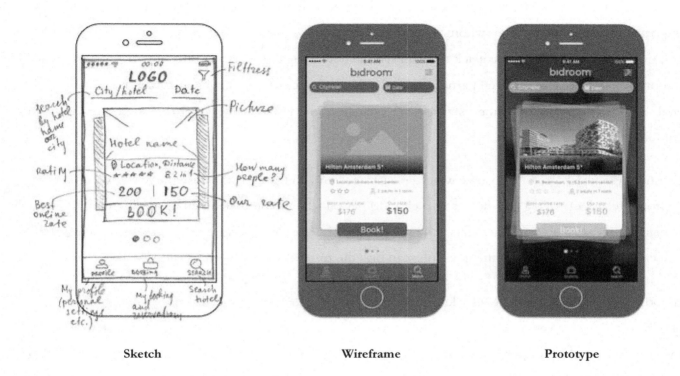

| Sketch | Wireframe | Prototype |
| --- | --- | --- |

1. A **sketch,** a hand drawing of the basic look that shows the basic functions of the product, will visually represent your product in an easy way.
2. A **wireframe**, also known as a page schematic or screen blueprint, is a visual guide that represents the skeletal framework of an app, software interface, or website.
3. A **prototype** appears highly similar to the envisioned final product, and mimics the basic functionality of the final product.

## Step 6: Test your MVP with customers.

Once you have your MVP prototype ready, it will be time to test it with customers. In this step, it is important that the people from whom you are soliciting feedback are in your target market. If you don't, you risk receiving customer feedback that can send you iterating in the wrong direction. A screener, which is a short survey to ensure research participants have the attributes of your target customer, helps achieve this goal. You can then schedule time to speak with each customer individually, either face to face or via video conference.

During these tests, carefully observe what the customer says and does as they use the MVP. When appropriate, ask clarifying questions to develop deeper understanding. Asking questions is an important skill to gain the most value from user tests. A good moderator will avoid asking leading questions such as, "That was easy, wasn't it?" Such leading questions can bias the response from the customer.

A good interviewer will also avoid asking closed questions such as, "Do you like that feature?" Such questions mandate a yes or no response from the user, an answer which doesn't provide much insight. Instead, you should ask open-ended questions such as "Could you please tell me what you thought of that feature?" Non-leading, open-ended questions give customers latitude in their answers and also encourage them to tell you more, thus giving you more helpful information.

It's beneficial to conduct user tests in batches or waves. A wave of five to eight users strikes a good balance between too few response, a situation which runs the risk of not detecting key issues, and too many responses, a situation which can lead to repetition and the low incremental value of additional tests. At the end of the wave, review all of the feedback you've received, both positive and negative. Identify patterns of similar feedback from many customers and prioritize any customer concerns that you've uncovered so that you can address them.

# Final Step: Iterate to Improve Product-Market Fit

The Lean Product Process is an iterative process. After analyzing the customer feedback in step six, revise your hypotheses based on what you have learned and loop back to an earlier step in the process (as you would in a flow chart). The feedback will determine which step you should return to next. If you only need to improve your UX design, then you can simply return to step five and proceed from there. But if your hypotheses about feature set, value proposition, underserved customer needs, or target customer base need to change, then you would return to the earliest step that requires revision and proceed from there.

In each iteration of the process, you will end up revising your MVP prototype, which you test again with a new wave of target customers. From one iteration to the next, you should ideally see an increase in positive feedback from customers and a decrease in negative feedback. You may find that you just can't seem to make much progress despite trying several iterations. If that happens, you should take a step back and revisit your hypotheses. You may conclude that in order to achieve higher levels of product-market fit you need to pivot (change one or more of your major hypotheses).

Ideally, after repeating the Lean Product Process for additional waves, you iterate to an MVP prototype that customers have limited or no negative feedback on, consider easy to use, and find very valuable. At that point, you have validated your key hypotheses and have designed a product with strong product-market fit and should feel comfortable investing the resources required to build the product. Following this process should give you a high degree of confidence that when you launch your product, customers will use it and find it valuable.

# Worksheet for
# The Startup Analysis Canvas Project
# Phase 1 - Value Propositions

Each of the phases build on one another, as they're all connected to the same new product or service idea. In this phase, you will craft the Value Propositions for your new startup company by identifying and analyzing a problem, your competition, and your target customers.

## 1. Define the Problem

The problem that you are defining is the basis of the startup company that you will design. Be sure to consider problems that can be solved with products or services that you can create or lead the creation of with a team that you can build. Startup ideas may include mobile apps, software, hardware, or related technologies that serve as the foundation, or key differentiation factor, of the startup.

- What is the problem that your team aims to solve?
- What evidence supports that the problem exists?
- List at least five articles, reports, or related research sources that support your claims in APA format.
  - Write a brief summary of the key findings from the aforementioned five or more references.
- Is the problem Urgent?
  - Is it one of the top few priorities for your target customer(s)?
- Is the problem Underserved?
  - Is there an absence of viable solutions to the problem that you aim to solve?

- Is the problem Unworkable?
    - Does your solution fix a broken situation or process in which there are real, measurable consequences to inaction?
- Is fixing the problem Unavoidable?
    - Is it driven by a mandate with implications associated with governance or regulatory control?
- Is the problem Conspicuous?
    - Why or why not?
- Is the problem Critical?
    - Why or why not?

## 2. Determine Your Target Customer

- Who is your target customer(s)?
    - This is the first step to defining your market and understanding the problem, need, or desire.
    - Analyze industries, markets, and value innovations to narrow the focus to real customers.
- What are their needs and wants?
    - Focus on customer value first.
    - Why do they need your product?
    - What benefits will they gain?
    - Can they make money or save money with your product?
    - Can they save time with your product?
    - Are there any other benefits?

- Are there enough people who care for you to be financially successful by solving this problem?
    - If you have a real customer and if you can deliver real value, then ask how many people experience these problems now?
    - How many might in the future?

## 3. Define Your Value Proposition

- What is unique about your solution to this problem?
    - What unique combination of discontinuous innovation, defensible technology, and/or disruptive business model are you bringing to market?
- What gains are you providing to your target customer(s)?
- What pains will your target customer(s) experience in adopting your product or service?

## 4. Design Your Minimum Viable Prototype

- Who are your current competitors?
- What market(s) do current competitors target?
- What are your current competitors' strengths?
- What are your current competitors' weaknesses?
- What are the minimum viable features of your product or service?
- Why are these features highly valuable for customers, and why are they rare among existing competitors?
- Using the format of "For (target customers) who are dissatisfied with (the current alternative), our product/service is a (new product/service) that provides (key problem-solving capability) unlike (the product alternative)," what is your value proposition?
    - Your answer to this question should be one sentence where you replace the text in parentheses with your responses.

# 3.0 TEAM STRATEGY

Within the Startup Analysis Canvas, the team strategy is the second category to analyze, paying attention to the founders, advisers, and partners.

## The Startup Analysis Canvas - Focus on Team Strategy

| 1 Value Proposition | | 2 Team Strategy | |
|---|---|---|---|
| | Problem | | Founders |
| | Competition | | Advisers |
| | Product-Market Fit | | Partners |

| 3 Market Strategy | | 4 Financial Strategy | |
|---|---|---|---|
| | Price | | Revenue Model |
| | Placement | | Cost Model |
| | Promotion | | Sales Model |
| | | | Funding Model |

Building your startup team is one of the most important activities that you will engage in as an entrepreneur. While entrepreneurs spend significant time in designing their product or service, they often spend surprisingly little time in designing their team. What should be a strategic decision is all too often led by which friends are interested in working with the startup or appear to be fun and/or smart. This strategy is not the way to build a high performing team. Instead, address the following key questions to avoid the pitfalls of team building, and maximize the likelihood of success for you, your team, and your startup:

# Who is involved in creating and selling your first products?

The typical initial team structure in today's agile, high-performance startups is:

- One to three co-founders with complementary skills and a common interest in the startup's mission
- Membership in an incubator environment, such as a university-based entrepreneurship program or a local co-working space
- Several active advisers that bring experience, wisdom, and relationships to the team
- Multiple startup peers that you can learn from and share with
- Minimal investment of $0 to $100,000

To establish this structure and determine who should be on your team, know that an early major goal is to build and test the functional prototype, the MVP. Your team needs to be able to understand the value proposition elements discussed earlier in the book and have the ability to build and test the MVP to achieve product-market fit. This process typically involves:

- Building the prototype and developing an alpha (i.e. a sellable first version) in three to six months
- Developing the minimal critical feature set to get customers to actually use the alpha product
- Improving design and usability to enhance the customer experience
- Setting up conversion metrics to understand how customers respond to your marketing and sales
- Achieving small-scale customer adoption. If your product is a large piece of expensive hardware, ten or so initial customers may be a viable goal. Alternatively, if your business model will ultimately require hundreds of thousands of customers, like an app or software as a service, hundreds or thousands of initial adoptions is the goal.

The primary goals for your team in the first three to six months are to

- Demonstrate the product or service concept
- Reduce product risk
- Test functional use
- Develop metrics
- Collect data to support future fundraising efforts

## Who is your Minimum Viable Team?

A successful team is comprised of persons with different skills with specific role players. As is the case with most team sports, you need different people with different skills to make the team work. 500 Startups suggest three roles for your startup team:

- **Hacker:** An engineer and developer who can build the functional prototype and alpha.
- **Hipster:** A person with design and user experience (UX) know-how to improve UX and conversion.
- **Hustler:** The business/sales/marketing person who can find a way to sell the product or service, scale customer acquisition, and distribute the product or service.

While these three roles need to be assigned in your team, preferably to two or three people including you, it's fine if you do not have extensive experience in these areas. Most startup teams have

- Limited (if any) professional experience
- Limited (if any) money
- Limited (if any) professional connections
- No experience in launching and growing a successful startup

These perceived "limits" were present for thousands of successful startups including Dell, Dropbox, Facebook, Google, Kinko's, Microsoft, Reddit, Snapchat, Squarespace, WordPress, and Yahoo.

## What business are you in?

In building your minimum viable team and your overall organizational structure of employees and partners, it's important to establish what business you are in. What activities will be your focus, and what activities will you achieve through partners?

What are the most important activities that you must perform in order to fulfill your specific value propositions? These activities are critical to a company reaching its target customer segments, sustaining its customer relationships, and ultimately creating long-term revenue streams. Key activities will vary based on the business model of the company carrying out the activity. Hence, an organization that relies heavily on its third party contracts will list channel management as a key activity. A product-driven business will lend Activities such as continuous research to better understand users and constant innovation in technology will be more significant for product-driven businesses.

A key activity for Microsoft is software development. For computer manufacturer Dell, supply chain management is a key activity. For a consulting business like McKinsey, solving client problems is a key activity.

## Questions to Consider

When evaluating your activities and team, it is essential to take a holistic view of the business to understand how the team will contribute to your activities.

**Based on your value propositions, what kinds of activities are key to your startup?**

**What kinds of activities are key to your distribution channels?**

**What kinds of activities are important to develop and maintain customer relationships?**

**What kinds of activities are fundamental to your revenue streams?**

# Typical Startup Activities for the Team to Lead

Your activities create a bridge between your value propositions and the target customer segment's needs and wants. Typical activities that are commonly practiced by most startups are research and development, production, marketing, sales, and customer service.

**Research & Development (R&D)**

The typical functions of research and development are:

- *New Product Research:* Before a new product can be produced, it must first be researched and developed. Research will be needed to explore what the design of the product should be, as well as expected production costs and the length of time it will take to produce sufficient amounts of the product. R&D should examine how much customers want or need the product in collaboration with the marketing team.

- *New Product Development:* The research phase can lead to the product being developed because the results achieved from the research phase were positive. Or research may indicate that the imagined product may not be successful in the market and should not be produced.

- *Existing Product Updates:* As you grow, R&D examines existing products to see if they require an upgrade based on evolving consumer needs or new entrants into the product category in the market.

- *Quality Checks:* R&D is involved in conducting quality checks to make sure that the products are working as intended.

- *Innovation:* The R&D team is also responsible for keeping an eye on innovations and new trends within the industry and ensuring that their product stays abreast of these trends.

**Production**

Production management consists of a number of activities which are outlined below. If you are partnering or outsourcing these activities, they may be performed by someone outside of your team. However, your team still needs to understand these activities in order to manage them effectively and to be sure that your partner is correctly delivering on your agreement.

- *Selection of Product and Design:* The first step is to select the right product and the right design for the product. This is a crucial decision because the combination of the right product (Value Proposition) and the right design will dictate the success or the failure of the company. Value engineering and value analysis are parts of this activity.
- *Selection of Production Process:* This stage consists of deciding what production process the organization will be using including the right technology, machines, inventory management system, and the like.
- *Selecting the Right Production Capacity:* The production management must have full knowledge of the expected demand for the product and set the production capacity accordingly, since either a dearth or a surplus of the product may lead to problems for the company. Break-even analysis is the most popular tool used by production managers to predict capacity.
- *Production Planning:* The production manager must decide on the routing and scheduling of the product. Routing is aimed at creating a smooth flow of work by discovering the easiest and most economical flow. Scheduling, on the other hand, refers to the timing of activities by mentioning a start and end time for each.
- *Production Control:* The production manager is also responsible for monitoring and controlling the production process. This is done by comparing planned production with actual production, exploring deviations—if any—and ultimately correcting these deviations to meet planned production.

- *Quality and Cost Control:* In today's economically driven world, consumers want the maximum quality for the cheapest price, access to the internet, and a world of options make them more discerning and fickle. Hence, it falls on the production manager to not only ensure that he is continuously improving the quality of the product, but also to reduce costs so their product can remain competitive in the market in terms of price.

- *Inventory Control:* Inventory Control is fundamental to a production-driven business because it prevents overstocking or understocking. Overstocking means the company will spend on materials that will ultimately go to waste. Understocking will affect production and result in late deliveries.

- *Maintenance and Replacement of Machines:* The production manager must consistently monitor the condition of the machines under his supervision by checking them and scheduling regular maintenance like oiling, replacing worn parts, and cleaning. This function ensures that there are no unexpected breaks in production.

**Marketing**

Marketing activities ensure the growth of the company by ensuring that consumers know of the startup's existence and evangelizing the value it provides to its customers. The functions of the marketing department include the following:

- *Strategy:* The marketing team is responsible for drafting and getting approval for a marketing strategy for the company, a strategy based on the company's overarching goals and missions before disseminating this strategy to the team and creating goals based on it.

- *Market Research:* The marketing team must have full knowledge of the market in which the company is operating, including the strengths and weaknesses of the product according to the customer, potential competitors in the market to whom the company may lose market share, and weaker competitors from whom company can acquire market share.

- *Product Development:* The marketing team works in conjunction with the product development team by identifying possible gap areas in the market for which the company can develop a product to address an unmet need. They are the ones with their fingers on the pulse of customers and a source of insight into consumer needs and feelings. Once the product is developed, the marketing team is also involved in pricing the product.

- *Communications:* The marketing team is responsible for all communication that is sent market regarding the product. The nature of this communication varies from press releases to online product reviews, advertisements, e-mails, among others.

- *Sales Support:* Marketing also works closely with the sales team by providing them with customer leads and promotional materials for potential customers.

- *Events:* Marketing is also responsible for organizing and executing events like seminars, product launches, and exhibitions. They will invite key or prospective customers to such events as well.

## Sales & Customer Services

Sales and customer service play a key role in the purchase and post-purchase experience of the customer. This team is key to ensuring that you build a cadre of repeat customers who will become your advocates in the market and drive more business to your company through word of mouth. Conversely, these customers can also be extremely vocal if they have suffered a bad customer experience and therefore can just as easily drive business away. Hence, one of the most crucial weapons in your arsenal is your sales and customer services team. They fulfill the following responsibilities on behalf of your company:

- *Handling Problems:* Customer service representatives generally assists customers with complaints. The breadth of their authority is dependent on company policy, but their core task is to ensure that when an irate customer calls, they do everything, within the scope of their job description, to leave the customer happy and satisfied. Customer representatives may be empowered to solve the problem on the spot by providing a replacement or refund. Others may act as gatekeepers who take information and then route it to the relevant departments.

- *Assisting in Sales:* Customer representatives are also critical to increasing the sales of the organization. They may do this by educating customers on the value propositions the product offers. Others may use upselling by persuading customers who call in to upgrade their services for improved quality.

- *Clerical Tasks:* You may include administrative and clerical tasks within the role of the customer services representative. Representatives may be routing calls to relevant support departments, maintaining a record of customer accounts—including new customers, and recording any changes that occur in these accounts.

In our next chapter, we will examine how to select and manage the founding team. In subsequent chapters, we will discuss the extended team of advisers and partners. All play a pivotal role in your team strategy.

# 3.1 FOUNDERS

It's unlikely that you have all of the necessary skills to accomplish everything that is necessary to build and launch a startup. Even if you believe that you have the skills, you will benefit tremendously by having help in developing your vision and help in making it a reality.

Hiring employees, or outsourcing work, is an option, although this requires money as well as time to manage that work. The majority of early-stage entrepreneurs do not have the money or the time to hire or outsource at the start of the startup.

Finding one or more co-founders is typically the best avenue to building the initial team, in lieu of hiring or outsourcing.

## Where do you find co-founders?

While friends or family may be accessible and perhaps interested in joining you, they typically lack the experience and commitment necessary to be a valuable co-founder. They also bring pre-existing personal relationships that may complicate the professional relationship, particularly since disagreements and conflicts in professional decisions can impact personal decisions and vice versa.

For student entrepreneurs, seeking fellow students is a proven method for securing co-founders. You can also reconnect with contacts from prior courses, internships, and jobs. If you were impressed with someone's energy and capabilities in a prior classroom or work role, you may reconnect to check their interest and availability to collaborate on your startup.

Meetups like Startup Weekend, conferences, entrepreneur forums, and local business organizations are useful to meet prospective co-founders. Online, you can also join entrepreneur groups on LinkedIn and Facebook or interact with people who meet your criteria on Twitter.

**Meet Prospective Co-founders at Startup Weekend**

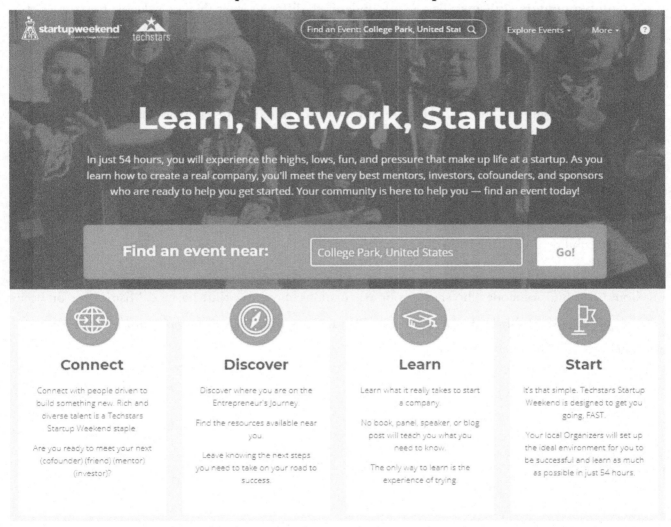

# What are the prerequisites for co-founders?

What matters most in selecting your co-founders? Successful startups typically emphasize two qualities:

- **Complementary skillsets:** Find a co-founder with different skills that are valuable for your startup. CEO (business) and CTO (technology) are common starting roles. You might also consider finding someone for CMO (sales and marketing) as well as Director roles.
- **Shared vision and values:** Shared vision is difficult to identify, but crucial for compatibility. Why are you all doing this startup? What are your goals for this startup? How do you measure success for yourselves? Shared goals are critical to compatibility.

Startup life is never boring. You could be hiring an employee in the morning, pitching your business to investors in the afternoon, and taking out the trash at the end of the day. A company's founders must be masters of flexibility, possessing the willingness to do almost anything at almost any time.

You should also find someone who shares your expectations about work-life balance. Mismatches on hours or effort quickly and reliably lead to resentments. Plan to be in the office at the same times. Make sure you share a view on how much you will work.

# What are the key traits of co-founders?

Startups are not for the faint of heart, weak of will, or slow of pace. Growth takes energy. Scaling takes energy. Survival takes energy. Choose someone who has the physical and mental energy to pull through the tough times, hang on through the slow times, and grow at all times. Seek traits that are aligned with the startup lifestyle, including

- **Eagerness to learn:** A good co-founder isn't someone who has life figured out or someone who believes he knows everything already. The people best suited for the startup life are those who want to learn more.

- **Self-sufficiency:** Seek a co-founder who is fully reliable and functions effectively with limited input from you. You should not have to spend time managing your co-founder's activities.

- **Empathy:** You're both working long hours. You're both dealing with problems. Knowing when your co-founder needs a boost is an extremely underrated skill. No one can do it on her own, especially without being able to empathize with those on your team.

- **Emotional intelligence:** Emotional intelligence is the ability to identify and manage your own emotions. Success in life is built upon the ability to effectively manage emotions. Startup life gives you plenty of reasons to lose your cool, fly off the handle, or crumple into a whimpering heap of emotions. Startup success demands that you stay calm and carry on.

- **Ability to work through disagreement**: Be prepared for differences of opinions and disagreements. Can you work through disagreements calmly? If your first few conflicts are more difficult to get through than you'd anticipated, it might be time to take a hard look at the relationship before moving ahead together.

## Why is trust fundamental?

When you're founding a company, there are plenty of ways to embezzle funds, cheat and lie, or engage in nasty or illegal activities. Because this is true, it's important to find someone who is honest. Be straightforward about what you expect and desire in a co-founder, and insist upon one hundred percent honesty at all times.

Trust in each other. While it's trite to say that every great relationship is built on a foundation of trust, this is very true for co-founders. You have to trust that whoever is managing the other side of the business has your best interests at heart. This is why a shared vision and shared values are so important.

## Will you find the perfect co-founder?

It's unlikely that you will find the perfect co-founder. There are no perfect people, so there is no perfect co-founder. You may join with a complete flop. Don't worry. Life isn't over after your first startup or your first co-founder. Keep your head up. Join with another co-founder, and reorganize the company; or start another company.

# What systems and structures will you develop?

As a startup, you have the opportunity to practice strategic leadership from day one. How your founding team approaches decision making, transparency, and innovation will influence your success each day. Use these three principles as a guide:

## 1. Distribute Responsibility

Strategic leaders gain their skill through practice, and practice requires a fair amount of autonomy. Founders should push power downward, across the organization, empowering people at all levels to make decisions. Distribution of responsibility gives potential strategic leaders the opportunity to see what happens when they take risks. It also increases the collective intelligence, adaptability, and resilience of the organization over time, by harnessing the wisdom of those outside the traditional decision-making hierarchy.

## 2. Be Honest and Open about Information

The management structure traditionally adopted by large organizations evolved from the military and was specifically designed to limit the flow of information. In that model, information truly equals power. The trouble is that when information is released to specific individuals on only a need-to-know basis, people have to make decisions in the dark. They do not know what factors are significant to the strategy of the enterprise; they have to guess. And it can be hard to guess correctly when you are not encouraged to understand the bigger picture or to question information that comes your way. Moreover, when people lack information, it undermines their confidence in challenging a leader or proposing an idea that differs from that of their leader.

Certain competitive secrets, such as products under development, may need to remain hidden. However, employees will benefit from a broad base of information, especially if they are to become strategic leaders. That is one of the principles behind "open-book management," the systematic sharing of information about the nature of the enterprise. Southwest Airlines, Harley-Davidson, and Whole Foods Market have all enjoyed sustained growth after adopting explicit practices of transparency.

Transparency fosters conversation about the meaning of information and the improvement of everyday practices. If productivity figures suddenly go down, for example, that could be an opportunity to implement change. Coming to a better understanding of the problem might be a team effort. It requires people to talk openly and honestly about the data. If information is concealed, it becomes tempting to manipulate the data to make it look better. The opportunity for strategic leadership is lost. Worse still, people are implicitly told that there is more value in expediency than in leading the company to a higher level of performance. Strategic leaders know that the real power in information comes not from hoarding it, but from using it to find and create new opportunities for growth.

## 3. Create Multiple Paths for Raising and Testing Ideas

Developing and presenting ideas is a key skill for strategic leaders. Even more important is the ability to connect their ideas to the way the company creates value. By setting up ways for people to bring their innovative thinking to the surface, you can help them learn to make the most of their own creativity.

This approach clearly differs from that of traditional cultures, in which the common channel for new ideas is limited to an individual's direct manager. The manager may not appreciate the value in the idea, may, in fact, block it from going forward and thereby stifle the innovator's enthusiasm. Of course, it can also be counterproductive to allow people to raise ideas indiscriminately without paying much attention to their development. Too many ideas, in too many repetitive forms, might then come to the surface, making it nearly impossible to sort through them all. The best opportunities could be lost in the clutter.

Instead, as your startup grows, create a variety of channels for innovative thinking. This may include cross-functional forums in which people can present ideas to a group of like-minded peers and test them against one another's reasoning. There could also be apprenticeships in which promising thinkers, early in their careers, sign on for mentorships with leaders who are well equipped to help them build their skills. You may setup in-house courses or sponsor attendance at university events. Reverse mentoring, in which junior staff members share their knowledge of new technology as part of a collaboration with a more established staff members, can also be effective.

Google has made use of a number of channels to promote innovation. Employees can directly email any of the leaders across the organization. The company has established "Google cafés" to spark conversation by encouraging interaction among employees and across teams. Executives hold weekly meetings with all of the employees to give workers at every level in-person access to senior leaders. People at Google learn to make the most of these opportunities. They know the conversations will be tough, but that genuinely worthwhile innovative thinking will be recognized and rewarded.

# What people, policies, and practices will you integrate?

Startups benefits from unconventional ways of thinking about assessment, hiring, and training.

## Make it Safe to Fail

A company's espoused statement of values may encourage employees to fail fast and learn fast. That may work until there is an actual failure that leads to a real loss. A dreaded phone call in the corporate world may follow. It's the one that begins with, "Who authorized this decision?" Big failures are simply unacceptable within most companies. Those who fail often suffer in terms of promotion and reward, if not worse.

You must enshrine acceptance of failure and willingness to admit failure early in the practices and processes of the startup, including the appraisal and promotion processes. For example, return-on-investment calculations need to assess results in a way that reflects the agreed-upon objectives, which may have been deliberately designed to include risk. Leaders should not learn only from efforts that succeed. They need to recognize the types of failures that turn into successes. They also need to learn how to manage the tensions associated with uncertainty and how to recover from failure in order to try new ventures again.

## Provide Access to Other Strategists

As your startup grows, give potential strategic leaders the opportunity to meet and work with their peers inside and outside of the company. Otherwise, they will remain hidden from one another and may feel isolated or alone. Once they know that there are others in the company with a similar predisposition, they can be more open and adept in raising the strategic value of what they do.

The first step is to find these internal strategists. Strategic leaders may not be fully aware themselves that they are distinctive. But it may be that others on their team recognize their unique talents. They may use phrases like "she just gets it," "he always knows the right question to ask," or "she never lets us get away with thinking and operating in silos" to describe them. A good way to learn about candidates is to ask, "Who are the people who really seem to understand what the organization needs and how to help it get there?" These may be people who aren't traditionally popular. Their predisposition to question, challenge, and disrupt the status quo can unsettle people, particularly people at the same level as they.

Of course, you don't want to create the impression that some people deserve special treatment. Instead, cultivate the idea that many managers, perhaps even most, have the potential to become strategic leaders. Then bring the first group together. Invite them to learn from one another and to explore ways of fostering a more strategic environment in the rest of the enterprise.

**Hire for Transformation**

Hiring decisions should be based on careful considerations of capabilities and experiences and should aim for diversity to overcome the natural tendency of managers to select people similar to themselves.

Test how applicants react to specific, real-life situations. Understand how they performed in previous companies and organizations. Conduct interviews that delve deeper than usual into candidates' psyches and abilities to empathize, their skills in reframing problems, and their agility in considering big-picture questions as well as analytical data.

You're looking for their ability to manage the minutiae of specific skills and practices, while also being visionary about strategic goals. The better they are at keeping near and far points of view simultaneously available, the better their potential to be strategic leaders within the company.

For those hired, the on-boarding processes should send explicit signals that they can experiment, take on more responsibility, and do more to help transform the organization than they could in their previous careers. They need to feel that the culture is open to change and to diverse views.

## How will you develop your skills to lead?

Founders should strive to be better strategic leaders each day. These tactics can help to prepare you for this personal evolution:

**Bring Your Whole Self to Work**

Strategic leaders understand that to tackle the most demanding situations and problems, they need to draw on everything they have learned in their lives. They want to tap into their full sets of capabilities, interests, experiences, and passions to come up with innovative solutions. And they don't want to waste their time in situations that don't align with their values.

Significantly, they encourage the people who report to them to do the same. In so doing, strategic leaders create lower-stress environments because no one is pretending to be someone else; people take responsibility for who they truly are. This creates an honest and authentic environment in which people can share their motivations and capabilities, as well as the enablers and constraints in their lives.

**Find Time to Reflect**

Strategic leaders are skilled in what organizational theorists Chris Argyris and Donald Schön call "double-loop learning." Single-loop learning involves thinking in-depth about a situation and the problems inherent in it. Double-loop learning involves studying your own thinking about the situation — a kind of meta-analysis of the biases and assumptions you have and the "undiscussables" that are too difficult to raise.

Your goal in reflection is to raise your game in double-loop learning. Question the way in which you question things. Solve the problems inherent in the way you problem-solve. Start with single-loop learning and then move to double-loop learning by taking the time to think. Ask yourself such questions as, "Why did I make that decision?" "What are the implications?" "What would I do differently next time?", and "How am I going to apply this learning going forward?"

Reflection helps you learn from your mistakes, but it also gives you time to figure out the value of your aspirations and whether you can raise them higher. It allows you the chance to spot great ideas using what you are already doing or things that are going on in your life. Managers are often caught up in the pressures of the moment. A mistake or a high-pressure project can feel overwhelming. But if you take a minute to step back and reflect on these problems, the process can provide the space to see what you did right.

Select reflections are more productive than others. Psychologists warn about "rumination," or dwelling on deceptive messages about your own inadequacies or the intractability of problems in a way that reinforces your feeling of being stuck. To avoid this pattern, deliberately give yourself a constructive question to reflect on. For example, ask yourself, "What are the capabilities we need to build next?" and "How can I best contribute?" Human capital teams can help by training individuals in these practices and ensuring that all managers support their team members who take the time to reflect.

### Recognize Leadership Development as an Ongoing Practice

Entrepreneurial leaders have the humility and intelligence to realize that their learning and development is never done. They admit that they are vulnerable and don't have all the answers. This characteristic has the added benefit of allowing other people to be the experts in some circumstances. In that way, entrepreneurial leaders make it easy for others to share ideas by encouraging new ways of thinking and asking for advice.

A thirst for learning gives potential entrepreneurial leaders the flexibility to be open to less obvious career opportunities in new industries, different types of roles, lateral moves, or stretch assignments.

In time, you may advance to the point where you are not concerned solely with your own role as an entrepreneurial leader, but also with cultivating opportunities for others. This will require a clear-eyed, reflective view of the talent around you.

By following the principles outlined here, you will give yourself the skill and influence to pave the way for others who follow. This is important because the ability to transform amid societal and business challenges and disruptions is essential to your company's success and perhaps even to its survival.

Lastly, be sure to create an operating agreement for your founders.

An Operating Agreement allows you to define the roles and responsibilities that each of your founders will play in the creation and growth of your company. You should seek legal counsel to develop such an agreement.

# 3.2 ADVISERS

A startup adviser is an individual who provides advice on running your startup successfully. Unlike a Board of Directors that has decision-making control for you and your startup, an adviser's suggestions may be accepted or declined.

The right advisers can dramatically improve your startup. Advisers can assist you in reaching your startup goals more quickly, and achieving success sooner. You can leverage the skills and relationships of experienced professionals. Their affiliation can also endorse your startup and elevate your credibility.

Advisers bring advice, ideas, lessons learned, contacts, and other such aid. An adviser's experience counts, and it helps you to run your startup better. Acquiring the right advisers and forming a proper advisory board is a critical early step in building your startup.

# Preparing for advisers

These questions will assist you in preparing for advisers:

- **What do you need right now?** The complexity of successfully launching a startup calls for a set of advisers who can assist with making things happen. Whether it's a targeted introduction or advice on user acquisition, be sure you know exactly what you need from the adviser you're seeking.

- **Do they care about your space?** Startups frequently target advisers who are popular or successful in a particular area. While this is usually an indication that an adviser has something to offer, it's important to do your research before reaching out. Be sure that your prospective adviser cares about both the industry you're in and the specific problem you're attempting to solve.

- **Are you prepared to answer tough questions?** A good adviser is like a good investor. Good advisers ask tough questions before diving in. Think through every aspect of your business and be prepared for the tough questions. Advisers' questions come from a desire to be ethical about accepting compensation rather than wanting to scare you away.

- **What are you hoping to gain?** Nothing spoils an otherwise good partnership faster than misaligned expectations. Be clear with the prospective adviser about what you want him to do and what you intend to get from him. Ask him what he hopes to gain as well.

- **How will you compensate the adviser?** Most advisers receive equity in exchange for their participation. For an early stage startup, this may be from a quarter of a percent to one percent of the equity in your company.

## How to select advisers

Too often, entrepreneurs fall into the trap of chasing big names as advisers. That's not the right strategy. They are some of the busiest people in the world, and even if such a person wanted to help you, she probably wouldn't be able to dedicate enough time to you.

Instead, try to find people who have domain expertise in whatever it is that you are trying to do. For example, if you are doing an e-commerce startup, find someone with experience in scaling e-commerce companies. A person like that will be much more valuable to you than some big name who has never done anything in e-commerce.

If you are a first-time entrepreneur who doesn't have any background or relationships in the startup world, recruiting one or two advisors who are respected in the startup world will gain you a certain level of credibility. Most importantly, these advisors will become voices of wisdom that you can rely on as you try to navigate unchartered territory.

As your startup grows, your needs will change, as will the types of advisors that you should recruit. The key to success in this arena is knowing what you don't know and finding advisors who are strong in your areas of weakness. For instance, if you are entering the enterprise sales market and no one on your team has experience in enterprise sales, seek an adviser with the experience and connections to help.

Once you have a candidate adviser interested in joining your advisory board, how do you know if they will be a fit or not? Use this list to help make that decision.

- **Excitement for Your Idea:** You want someone who is as excited about your startup as you are. That's what gets people motivated to help you beyond what's necessary.

- **A Passion for Something Other Than Making Money:** Increased revenue and profitability are byproducts of honesty, hard work, thought leadership, and authentic passion for your trade. Find someone who's not willing to sacrifice those most scalable attributes while they advise.

- **Experience:** Seek experience in the trenches of business. If you have someone who's been where you want to go and can help you avoid pitfalls, you're saving yourself a lot of headaches.

- **Deep Industry Knowledge:** At least one adviser should have strong industry expertise. A large professional network and deep industry knowledge will help you to avoid making major mistakes.

- **Commitment:** Many people can be initially excited by a concept. You need to find people whose backgrounds demonstrate that they maintain commitments.

- **An Action-Oriented Personality:** Be certain that the adviser translate their advice into action and that they are interested in being actively engaged in your startup.

- **Communication Skills:** Communication skills are essential. If they can't communicate advice or communicate it badly, that advice won't help you succeed.

- **Networking Skills:** Appreciate how important it is to have a strategic adviser who can connect you with the right people and resources to help expand your company smarter and faster.

- **Culture Fit:** If the advisers of the company don't understand the personality, passion, and purpose of the startup they're helping, their advice is likely to miss the mark.

- **The Ability to Tell the CEO That She Is Wrong**: It is not only important to have contrasting views, it's important to tell the executive team that they feel they are headed in the wrong direction.

# How to manage advisers

Managing expectations is one of the most important parts of building a successful advisory relationship. Start with a base expectation of how often you'd like to meet. You typically can't expect more than a few hours a month. As your relationship grows, you will learn how to best communicate, how frequently you should communicate, what the best channels for communication are, and other important information of this sort. You will also go through waves when you will need one adviser more often than another. Be sure to keep all of your advisers up to date. Keep them informed and excited about being your advisers so that they can be helpful when you need them.

Managing your advisers, and yourself is central to the success of the relationship. Beyond expectations setting, be sure to:

- **Ask.** Ask your advisers for their strategies, ideas, advice, contacts, etc. Keep in mind that they have their prior commitments and are never idle. If you ever want their help, you will have to ask them for it. You have to take the first step.

- **Be timely with payment.** If you're asking for helping and counting on an expert for advice, you should also be willing, or rather happy, to pay them for it (or share equity). Never delay payments, and make sure that you pay the exact amount of equities and remunerations as detailed in the contract.

- **Exercise mutual respect.** Every relationship is based on mutual respect. Ensure that you are respectable toward your advisers. Ensure that you are getting the same respect. Although many advisors come with more experience and success than the entrepreneurs, if you don't feel respected, don't waste your time with them.

## How to compensate advisers

Advisers typically do not work for free. And if they do, it's probably only for a few weeks. Expect to pay them by sharing equity (i.e. ownership) in your company. Alternatively, advisers may work on an hourly pay basis.

The specific amount of equity compensation for an adviser depends on the stage of your company, the amount of time you expect the advisor to spend with you, what you need them to do, and what the market rate is for their services. If you've not raised any significant funding for your company, you may compensate the adviser in a quarter of a percent to one percent of equity for up to a year of service. The further along in the growth path you are, the less equity you'd have to offer since the value of your company should be increasing.

## Developing the Founder-Adviser Agreement

To help entrepreneurs compensate their mentors for the time they dedicate to helping their businesses grow, the Founder Institute has developed a solution to this long-standing challenge that all startups experience. The Founder Adviser Standard Template was designed to provide founders and advisers with a simple legal framework to formalize their relationship without all of the legal chaos.

The Founder Adviser Standard Template is available from https://fi.co/FAST.

A proper advisory board is a minor investment and can increase the success and value of your startup. Don't be hesitant or afraid to ask people who are out of your realm.

# 3.3 PARTNERS

Beyond founders and advisers, partners are often a fundamental element of the team equation. In this chapter, we will explore ways to establish and manage partnerships. We'll also discuss how outsourcing can improve your success.

## What are the reasons for partnerships?

A starting point for establishing partnerships is to determine your reasons for partnerships. For most startups, these reasons may include the following:

- Access resources and skills beyond those of the startup,
- Develop new innovations and new products,
- Speed time to market,
- Access new markets, and/or
- Develop complementary products.

Partnerships can also allow you to maintain focus on your core competencies.

# What are the types of partnerships?

Once you've defined your reasons for partnerships, understanding the types of partnerships is valuable. Partnerships typically exist in one of two forms: horizontal partnerships or vertical partnerships.

- **Horizontal Partnerships** are formed between partners operating in the same business arena. The company partners with a competitive company to improve its position against other competitors. Horizontal partnerships may be seen as anti-competitive; hence, anti-trust laws should be taken into account before entering into this type of relationship. One type of productive partnership may be a shared research and development program between two firms, one which can result in the selling of a similar product to distinct geographic markets with each partner entering into a non-compete agreement.

- **Vertical Partnerships** are partnerships between firms and their suppliers or distributors. Some firms utilize vertical alliances to produce their products and services. Vertical alliances deepen the relationship between the firm and suppliers through the exchange of know-how and commercial intelligence. They extend the firm's network and benefit customers by lowering prices. Suppliers become actively involved in product design and distribution arrangements. The close bond between an automotive manufacturer and its suppliers is an example. A complementary vertical alliance is formed when the supplier agrees to work exclusively for the firm.

# What are the risks of partnering?

While there are significant benefits to partnering, associated risks may include:

- Loss of intellectual property, particularly trade secrets,
- Loss of autonomy and control,
- Lack of attention in managing the relationship, and/or
- Incompatible cultures.

# How can success be realized?

To minimize the risks of partnerships and position yourself for success, focus on these guiding principles:

- **Interdependence:** Shared mutual dependencies provide motivation for partnership success. Asymmetrical dependence leads to vulnerability and possible exploitation. Caution is warranted when working with partners of unequal size. Low levels of interdependence provide less shared motivation for the partnership to succeed.

- **Governance Structure:** Terms, conditions, systems, and processes are important. A unilateral structure means that one party has the authority to make decisions. In a bilateral structure, governance is based on mutual expectations regarding behaviors and activities.

- **Commitment:** Consider the desires of each partner to cultivate and continue the relationship. Committed members are less likely to take advantage and make decisions that sabotage the future viability of relationship.

- **Effective Communication:** Frequent sharing improves credibility and reliability. Sharing of this sort may include proprietary information. Develop a process for effective conflict resolution, and be judicious in the use of legal contracts. While contracts might seem to violate the spirit of cooperation, contracts can also clarify obligations and expectations.

- **Trust:** Ideally, each partner's decisions will serve the best interest of the partnership. Partners should act honestly and benevolently. Trust in the partner's motives and intents is crucial. Trust contributes to effective information sharing and elevates the sharing of ideas and resources.

The reasons for and types of partnerships are diverse and evolving. Use best practices to maximize the success and mitigate the risks of partnerships.

# What is outsourcing?

Partnerships and outsourcing have different traits that result in different consequential benefits and risks.

Partnerships may be simple agreements. They do not necessarily involve monetary payment from one company to another, or a binding contractual agreement between two companies.

Outsourcing is the contracting of service, typically through monetary means. The objective of outsourcing is often to minimize or limit the resources that would normally be required to perform business functions internal to the company. A company that outsources usually reduces its costs compared to performing these activities with their own employees and resources.

The following list includes types of outsourcing and examples:

- **Contract Manufacturing:** Production of Products
- **Business Process Outsourcing:** Call Centers
- **Information Technology Outsourcing:** Software Development
- **Innovation Outsourcing:** R&D or Product Design

## What are the models for outsourcing?

While offshoring is a popular model for outsourcing, there are a variety of models. These include:

- **Offshoring:** Performing functions outside of client's home country
- **Captive Offshoring:** Company-owned facilities in another country
- **Nearshore Outsourcing:** Outsource provider near company's own boundaries in the same time zone
- **Home Shoring:** Domestic outsourcing, hiring domestic workers in a person's own home
- **Farm Shoring:** Outsourcing to domestic, rural areas
- **Reverse Outsourcing:** An outsourced company opens an office in the original country.

## What are the reasons for outsourcing?

The reasons for outsourcing are similar to those for partnerships. Outsourcing presents startups with the opportunity to:

- Reduce expenses through contract manufacturing, economies of scale, volume discounts, and/or supply chain efficiencies
- Hone core competencies by outsourcing non-essential tasks and focusing on essential tasks
- Access the capabilities of outsource providers, which might have access to a skilled, lower-cost labor pool
- Mitigate human resource costs and management issues

# What are the risks of outsourcing?

While there are significant benefits to outsourcing, associated risks may include:

- Cost savings that don't materialize as planned since it's difficult to calculate true cost in advance
- Quality concerns due to suppliers not understanding customers' needs and/or not delivering as planned
- Over-dependence on outsourced vendor can harm a business if the vendor's operations are disrupted.
- Dilution of competitive advantage due to less differentiation from competitors that may use the same or similar vendors
- Risk of fostering new competition due to loss of differentiation and/or loss of trade secrets
- Public backlash that can result in political issues or other public relations problems

To mitigate these risks, a contingency approach to outsourcing is recommended. Start by asking these key questions:

- What specific benefits do you anticipate by outsourcing a specific activity?
- What are the strategic pros and cons of outsourcing rather performing that activity internally?
- Is the vendor capable of and reliable in completing the activity?
- Does your contract provide for appropriate oversight and accountability?

In summary, outsourcing presents a valuable avenue for new ventures to develop and launch products and services. Outsourcing exists in many types and forms. Risks from outsourcing can be mitigated through best practices in selecting and managing the relationships.

Partnerships and outsourcing present a valuable avenue for startups to develop and launch products and services.

Partnerships and outsourcing exist in many types and forms. Risk of partnerships and outsourcing can be mitigated through best practices in selecting and managing the relationships.

.

# Worksheet for
# The Startup Analysis Canvas Project
## Phase 2 – Team Strategy

Each of the phases build on one another, as they're all connected to the same new product or service idea. In this phase, you will craft the Team Strategy for your new startup company.

## 1. Founders

A successful team is comprised of persons with complementary (i.e., different) skills with specific role players. As is the case with most team sports, you need different people with different skills to make the team work. 500 Startups suggest three roles for your startup team:

- Hacker: An engineer and developer type person that can build the functional prototype (MVP) and alpha.
- Hipster: A person with design and user experience (UX) know-how to improve UX and conversion
- Hustler: The business/sales/marketing person who can find a way to sell the product or service, scale customer acquisition, and distribute the product or service

For your team, who are the hackers, the hipsters, and hustlers?

- List the names of each team member, their major(s) and minor(s), and their professional experiences (i.e., software developer for Google). This can be listed as bullets or in a table. Also, note who is a hacker, a hipster, or a hustler based on their skills, experiences, and interests.

Typical early activities for startups include research and development (R&D), production, marketing, and sales and customer service.

- Based on your categorization of your team into hackers, hipsters, and hustlers and with consideration of the four early activities for startups, is your team well comprised (i.e., is your team capable of creating and launching a startup company)?
    o If yes, discuss why you believe your team is well positioned for success.
    o If no, what capabilities is your team missing? It is likely that you are missing one or more role players.

Upwork is an online marketplace to identify freelancers interested in working with startups. There is no fee nor registration required to browse available freelancers. Go to https://www.upwork.com/, click in the Find Freelancers search box, and type what you are looking for (i.e., app developer). Filter the returns based on your interests. Perhaps you're interested in freelancers with an eighty percent job success rate or better and a low hourly rate.

- For each of the role players that you are missing, list the names and URLs from Upwork for the freelancers that you believe will be an asset to your team (not as a founder, but as a contracted employee).
- For each of the role players selected, describe why that freelancer would be an asset to your team based on the person's experience and skills.

## 2. Advisers

A startup adviser is an individual who provides advice on running your startup successfully. Advisers can assist in reaching your startup goals more quickly and sooner. You can leverage the skills and relationships of experienced professionals. The affiliation with an adviser can also endorse your startup and elevate your credibility. Acquiring the right advisers and forming a proper advisory board is a critical early step in building your startup. Seek advisers who have domain expertise in whatever it is that you are trying to do. For example, if you are creating an e-commerce startup, find someone with experience in scaling e-commerce companies. Five advisers is a reasonable number for startup teams.

- Based on the existing relationships among your team members, do you have five advisers in mind who could be highly valuable for your startup? For example, do you have a friend or family member with more than ten years of experience in your startup's industry, extensive relationships in your target market, significant technical expertise in the technologies that your startup uses, or the like?
  - If yes, list the name, employer, and job title of each adviser. It is unlikely that you can create an excellent advisory team based solely on your existing relationships. If you are in need of one or more advisers, that is fine and is typically the case for first time entrepreneurs.
  - If no, use LinkedIn to identify candidate advisers.
- Based on your LinkedIn adviser search, list the names and the LinkedIn URLs for the advisers that you believe will be an asset to your team.
  - You should list five advisers in this response.
- For each adviser selected, describe why that person would be an asset to your team based on his or her experience and skills.

## 3. Partners

Beyond founders and advisers, partners are often a fundamental element of the team equation. A starting point is to determine your reasons for establishing partnerships. These reasons may include access to resources and skills beyond those available to the startup, to develop new innovations and new products, to speed time to market, to access new markets, and to develop complementary products.

Based on your prior work on the Value Propositions and your analysis of your founders and advisers, what companies or organizations are candidates for partnerships?

- List at least five candidates, along with their URLs and compose one sentence to explain why you would benefit from partnering with them. Also include one sentence on why they would partner with you.
- Do not list companies that are on the Fortune 500 (http://fortune.com/fortune500/list), as it's very rare for these companies to partner with startups.
- For all partners selected, describe why that person would be an asset to your team.

Outsourcing is the contracting of services to companies, typically to minimize or limit the resources that would normally be required to perform business functions internally, thus reducing costs. Types of outsourcing and examples include contract manufacturing (i.e., production of products), business process outsourcing (i.e., call centers), information technology outsourcing (i.e., software development), and innovation outsourcing (i.e., R&D or product design).

- Based on your prior work on the Value Propositions, your analysis of your founders, and freelancers that you would hire directly, what activities could be performed well via outsourcing?
- Which company might serve in this outsourced role?
- List at least five companies along with their URLs.
- For each of outsourcing companies selected, describe why it would be an asset to your team.

# 4.0 MARKET STRATEGY

Within the Startup Analysis Canvas, the market strategy is the third category to analyze, paying attention to price, placement, and promotion.

## The Startup Analysis Canvas - Focus on Market Strategy

| 1 Value Proposition | Problem | 2 Team Strategy | Founders |
|---|---|---|---|
| | Competition | | Advisers |
| | Product-Market Fit | | Partners |

| 3 Market Strategy | Price | 4 Financial Strategy | Revenue Model |
|---|---|---|---|
| | Placement | | Cost Model |
| | Promotion | | Sales Model |
| | | | Funding Model |

Marketing is simplistically defined as "putting the right product in the right place, at the right price, at the right time." Significant research, analysis, and planning is required to develop and implement the strategy.

In this chapter, we will introduce the Four Ps, the history and purpose of the marketing mix concept and terminology, key features of the marketing mix, ways to develop the marketing mix, and an example of a marketing mix: Nivea.

# The Four Ps of Marketing

The use of the marketing mix is an excellent way to ensure that "putting the right product in the right place, at the right price, at the right time" will happen. The marketing mix is a crucial tool for understanding what the product or service can offer for planning a successful product offering. The marketing mix is most commonly executed through the Four Ps of marketing: Product, Price, Placement, and Promotion.

- **Product:** The product is either a tangible good or an intangible service that is seen to meet a specific customer need or demand. All products follow a logical product life cycle. It is vital for startups to understand and plan for these various stages and their unique challenges. Focus on understanding those problems that the product is attempting to solve. The benefits offered by the product and all of its features need to be understood. The unique selling proposition of the product needs to be studied. In addition, the potential buyers of the product need to be identified and understood.

- **Price:** Price encompasses the actual amount that the buyer is expected to pay for a product. How a product is priced will directly affect how it sells. This is linked to what the perceived value of the product is to the customer. If a product is priced higher or lower than its perceived value, then it will not sell optimally. This is why it is imperative to understand how a customer sees perceives your product or service. If there is a positive customer value, then a product may be successfully priced higher than its objective monetary value. Conversely, if a product has little value in the eyes of the consumer, then it may need to be underpriced to sell. Price may also be affected by distribution plans, value chain costs and markups, and the way that competitors price a rival product.

- **Placement:** Placement has to do with how the product will be delivered to the customer. Distribution is a key element of placement. The placement strategy will help assess what channel is the most suited to a product. How a product is accessed by the end-user also needs to complement the rest of the product strategy.

- **Promotion:** The marketing communication strategies and techniques all fall under the promotion category. These strategies can include advertising, sales promotions, special offers, and public relations. Whatever the channel used, it is necessary for it to be suitable for the product, the price, and the end-user that it is being marketed to. It is important to differentiate between marketing and it's sub-category of promotion. Promotion is the communication aspect of the entire marketing function.

## The Marketing Mix Concept and Terminology

The marketing mix concept gained popularity following an article titled "The Concept of the Marketing Mix" by Neil Borden published in 1964. Borden explained how he started using the term, inspired by James Culliton, who in the 1940s described the marketing manager as a "mixer of ingredients." Borden's article detailed these ingredients as product, planning, price, branding, distribution, display, packaging, advertising, promotions, and personal selling, among others. Eventually E. Jerome McCarthy clustered these multiple items into four high level categories that we now know as the Four Ps of marketing. Its elements are the basic, tactical components of a marketing plan. Together, elements in these four categories help develop marketing strategies and tactics.

# Key Features of the Marketing Mix

The Four Ps were refined over the years by experts to ensure the creation and execution of a successful marketing strategy. The aim is to satisfy both the customer and the seller. When properly understood and utilized, the Four Ps dramatically enhance a product's success by focusing on these key features:

- **Interdependent Variables:** The marketing mix is made up of four unique variables. These four variables are interdependent and need to be planned in conjunction with one another to ensure that the action plans within all four are complimentary and aligned.

- **Specific Marketing Targets**: Through the use of the interdependent set of variables, the company aims to achieve specific marketing targets (i.e., awareness, adoption, revenues, profits, etc.).

- **Flexible Concept:** The marketing mix is a fluid and flexible concept. The focus on any one variable may be increased or decreased given unique marketing conditions and customer requirements.

- **Constant Monitoring:** It is vital to keep an eye on changing trends and requirements, within the company as well as in the market, to ensure that the elements in the marketing mix stay relevant and current.

- **Role of Marketing Manager:** A mature, intelligent, and innovative marketing manager needs to be at the helm of the marketing mix. This pivotal role means that this manager is responsible for achieving the desired results through the skill manipulation of these four main variables.

- **Customer as the Focal Point:** A vital feature of the marketing mix is that the customer is the focal point of the activities. The value of the product is determined by customer perceptions. The goal is to achieve a satisfied and loyal customer.

# Developing Your Marketing Mix

While intuition and creative thinking are valuable skills for marketing decisions in a startup, relying on these alone often leads to inaccurate assumptions and poorly developed strategies. To create a marketing mix that is based in research and combines facts with innovation, use a systematic process.

## Step 1: Defining the Unique Selling Proposition

The first item on the agenda should be to define what the product has to offer, its unique selling proposition. Through prospective customer interviews, the startup founder must identify how important this unique selling proposition is to the consumer and whether the consumer truly desires the product. It needs to be clearly understood what the key features and benefits of the product are and whether consumers will purchase the product or participate in the commercialization strategy for the startup.

## Step 2: Understanding the Consumer

The second step is to understand the consumer. The product can be focused by identifying the persons who will purchase it. All other elements of the marketing mix follow from this understanding. Who are the customers? What do they need? What is the value of the product to them? This understanding will ensure that the product offering is relevant and targeted to the right audience with the right features and at the right price.

## Step 3: Understanding the Competition

The next step is to understand the competition. The prices and related benefits such as discounts, warranties, and special offers need to be assessed. An understanding of the subjective value of the product and a comparison with its actual direct and indirect costs will help to set a realistic price point.

## Step 4: Evaluating Placement Options

At this point, the startup team needs to evaluate placement options to understand where the customer is most likely to make a purchase and what costs are associated with using this sales channel. Multiple channels may help target a wider customer base and improve ease of access. Alternatively, if the product serves a niche market, then it may make sense to concentrate distribution to a specific area or channel. The perceived value of the product is closely tied to the places where it is available for sale.

## Step 5: Developing Communication / Promotion Strategy

Based on the audience identified and the price points established, the marketing communication strategy can now be developed. Whatever promotional methods are finalized need to appeal to the target customers and ensure that the key features and benefits of the product are clearly communicated and highlighted.

## Step 6: Cross-check of the Marketing Mix

A step back needs to be taken at this point to see how all of the elements of the marketing mix relate to one other. All of the marketing mix variables are interdependent and rely on one other for a strong strategy. Do the proposed selling channels reinforce the perceived value of the product? Is the promotional material aligned with the planned distribution channels? The marketing plan can be finalized once it is clear that all four elements are in harmony and that there are no conflicting messages, either implicit or explicit.

# Marketing Mix Example – NIVEA

## The Company

NIVEA is a well-known company that is in the high quality skin and beauty care product market. NIVEA is one of the brands manufactured and sold by Beiersdorf, which was established in 1882. In the United Kingdom, the company has always focused on ensuring availability of their products to as many people as possible. In addition, the company has always strived to understand the varied needs of its vast consumer base and bring as many specific products to market as possible.

## Marketing Mix for a New Product Line

Market research revealed an opportunity in the market for a younger customer base. This led to the launch of Nivea Visage Young in 2005. This product was developed for girls aged thirteen to nineteen.

For the eventual launch of the product, the company needed to develop a balanced and relevant marketing mix to appeal to its young audience. Through its initial launch in 2005 and a subsequent relaunch in 2007, the company focused closely on the marketing mix balance to help ensure that all elements of the product appealed to the target audience in order to achieve success.

- Product: The company placed emphasis on ongoing research to understand the constantly evolving market and consumer dynamics. This knowledge helped the company to develop more innovative new products that fulfill consumer needs. It became clear that younger consumers wished for a more specific product that addressed the skin needs of their age category, that there was a felt need for a product that offered a beautifying regime for daily use, rather than a medicated product that targeted specific skin problems. The latter sorts of products were already more than readily available from competitors. The product was subsequently redesigned to meet these specialized requirements. From the company's perspective, some of the changes helped meet its commitment to the environment by including more efficient packaging to reduce waste, by using recyclable plastic, and by utilizing natural products in its manufacture.

- Price: An effective pricing strategy takes into account the product's perceived and actual values. The final price should be based on these in order to make the product attractive to the buyer and seller. After its relaunch, Nivea Visage Young was priced higher than before to account for the new formula, better packaging, and extended range of products. The price remained competitive for the value delivered to customers, who were typically mothers buying for their daughters. Effective pricing resulted in sales from this product accounting for seven percent of all Nivea Visage sales.

- Promotion: Nivea bases its promotions on the lifestyle of its target market. Their promotions are consumer-led through different below-the-line solutions. Sample sales are a key activity that allows consumers to try out the actual product. There is also an interactive online magazine *FYI* (an acronym which stands for fun, young, independent) to increase product visibility and association. The company has also maintained a strong social media presence on popular social media networks. This use of new media has ensured better brand awareness and association among its target audience.

- Placement: Nivea aims to have a wide reach for its products to ensure that it is easily available. The primary channels used are retail stores. High Street stores such as Boots and Superdrug account for nearly sixty-five percent of sales. Another portion of their sales comes from grocers. This covers young people making their own purchases (mostly High Street), as well as mothers buying for their daughters (mostly grocery stores). These stores ensure a cost effective distribution channel that has a wide reach. The company manages its own costs by selling to wholesalers rather than directly to smaller stores. It also does not sell online directly, but the product is sold through intermediaries.

## Conclusion

Through its successful use of a balanced marketing mix, Nivea Visage Young has managed to create a clear position in the market. It addresses a need felt by a specific niche segment. Traditional distribution methods are balanced by a unique product and updated promotional strategies. This ensures that the brand message reaches the right people at the right time in the right way.

As we see from the Nivea example, it is valuable for a startup to focus equally on all elements of the marketing mix while planning for a product. Eventually, there may be a need to divert more resources towards one variable such as strong distribution channels over promotional activities. First, there needs to be a clear plan and strategy decided upon. An effective marketing mix can mean the difference between an unsuccessful product and an incredible success.

# 4.1 PRICE

# How much should you charge for a new product?

Charge too much, and it won't sell. This problem can be fixed relatively easily by reducing the price.

Charging too little is far more dangerous. A startup not only forgoes significant revenues and profits, but also fixes the product's market value position at a low level.. Once a price is promoted in the market, it is difficult to raise because customers will be resistant to increasing prices.

Pricing plays a pivotal role in the marketing mix. The reason for its significance is that whereas the rest of the elements of the marketing mix are cost generators, price is the only source of income. Through pricing, the organization supports the cost of production, the cost of distribution, and the cost of promotion.

Simplistically, price is the value measured in financial terms for the exchange of a product or service. Pricing is a complicated element that reflects supply and demand, the actual value of the object, and the perceived value of the product or service in the mind of the consumer. A price that does not reflect these factors and is either too high or too low can lead to a lack of sales. This is why pricing will change according to circumstances and time.

The complexity of a company's pricing strategy is well evidenced by considering how Netflix's pricing strategy works as its profit margins improve. This requires an understanding of how to project the number of future buyers, which are Domestic Subscribers in Netflix's case, and the estimated revenues and costs associated with these buyers.

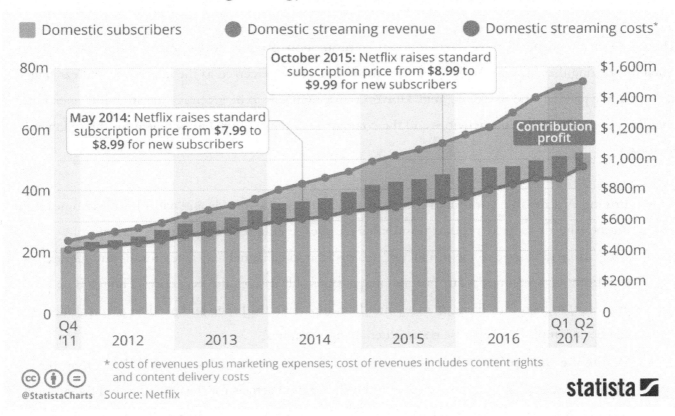

## Netflix's Pricing Strategy Works as Profit Margins Improve

■ Domestic subscribers     ● Domestic streaming revenue     ● Domestic streaming costs*

**October 2015:** Netflix raises standard subscription price from **$8.99** to **$9.99** for new subscribers

**May 2014:** Netflix raises standard subscription price from **$7.99** to **$8.99** for new subscribers

Contribution profit

* cost of revenues plus marketing expenses; cost of revenues includes content rights and content delivery costs

@StatistaCharts    Source: Netflix

statista

In the fall of 2011, Netflix was nearly break-even financially, meaning that its revenues nearly equals its costs. Their major costs include production, content rights, content delivery, marketing, etc. Netflix raised their pricing in May 2014, and again in October 2015, based on the popularity of its platform, increasing costs due to producing original content, and a host of other factors.

In this chapter, we will examine the importance of pricing, pricing objectives, types of pricing strategies, the way to price, and pricing issues.

# Why is pricing important?

There is often a tendency for marketers to focus on promotion, product development, and market research when prioritizing their responsibilities. These activities are often perceived as the interesting and exciting aspects of the product and marketing mix. However, pricing needs to be given its due attention since it has great impact on the rest of the activities and the company. Pricing is of vital importance for the following reasons:

- **Pricing is a flexible variable.** Pricing changes can be made quickly and with short lead times if the business needs to make product positioning changes or counter a competitor's activities. In comparison, a change to the product or to a distribution channel may take months and require significant costs. Similarly, any promotion decisions will also require new costs. Though it is important to plan for pricing changes and their impact on the brand and product perception, this can be accomplished faster than any other changes can be.

- **Define the right pricing**. Any pricing decisions for a product need to be made through proper research and analysis and be aligned with the strategic objectives for the company and the product. A decision made too quickly and with superficial assessment can result in a loss of revenue. A price below the perceived value can lead to a loss in additional revenue and a target audience that misjudges the quality of the brand through low price points. If this price is raised later, the existing customers may feel like they are being unfairly burdened. A price set too high can also result in potential buyers staying away altogether. In large companies, pricing decisions are often made by a team of experts who spend time conducting research that considers all of he variables of the market and brand. For startups, a pricing analysis should also be conducted by the team.

- **Pricing is a trigger for first impressions.** In many product categories, consumers will form perceptions about quality and relevance as soon as they see the price. Eventually, the decision to buy or not may be based on the perceived value of the product or marketing mix offering. There is always a danger that the first impression triggered by the price point will either make the rest of the offering irrelevant or bias the customer's assessment of the product.

- **Pricing is key to sales promotions.** Sales promotions are often a limited-time, price-based offering such as a percentage reduction or a two for one offer. These are meant to generate interest in the product or align with a special occasion or holiday. Used wisely, this can be a useful method of increasing sales, but startups should avoid the temptation to offer these special prices too often. In this scenario, buyers may delay purchasing the product or service until the next sales promotion.

# What are your pricing objectives?

Before any pricing decisions are made, a startup must establish what it aims to achieve through pricing. Often, these objectives include the following:

- **Profit Maximization:** Keeping in mind revenue and costs, a startup may want to maximize profits. Profit maximization objectives should be long-term and not focus only on the short-term.

- **Revenue Maximization:** With less focus on profits, a startup may focus on increasing revenues in order to increase market share and lower costs in the long-term.

- **Maximize Quantity:** A startup may want to sell a specific number of items to decrease long-term costs.

- **Maximize Profit Margin:** Another objective may be to increase the profit margin for each unit and not focus on the total number of units sold.

- **Quality Leader:** A startup may want to use price to signal high quality and establish itself as the quality leader.

- **Partial Cost Recovery:** If a startup has multiple revenue streams, it may not be too focused on recovering a hundred percent of its costs.

- **Survival:** At times, the best a startup can do is to cover costs and remain in the market. If the market is in decline or there are too many competitors, survival may take temporary priority over profit.

- **Status Quo:** There may be a need to avoid price wars with competitors. A startup might maintain a stable price to continue a stable profit level later.

# What is your range of pricing options?

For products that closely replicate competitors or offer small improvements, the room to maneuver with pricing is relatively narrow. Incremental approaches may come close to the optimal price. Charging just one percent less than the optimal price for a product can mean forfeiting eight percent of its potential operating profit. The more novel a product is, the more important it is for startups to take a broader view of the pricing possibilities.

## The Highest Price

Since incremental approaches tend to focus on the lower end of the price range, startups should start by defining the opposite end of the spectrum, the highest price at which a product can be sold, a concept called a price ceiling. This may ultimately prove to be unrealistic, as there may not be a sufficient market at that price level. It may leave too much room for competitors to enter at a lower price, or customers may be strong enough to demand a greater share of the value that the product creates and demand a lower price. However, establishing this price ceiling for debate with the startup team will ensure that each and every potential price point is brought up for discussion.

To establish a price ceiling, a clear understanding of a product's benefits for its customers is essential. The value of these benefits should be evaluated through market research.

Marketing tools including conjoint analysis and perceptual mapping can assess how much value each benefit offers to customers. Avoid relying exclusively on your internal perceptions, as these can skew your understanding of the market. While formulating the research and writing of the questions for customer interviews, a startup should ensure that they cover a broad range of topics.

To take an accurate measure of the benefits a product offers and thereby find its true price ceiling, market research must be designed to elicit more open-ended feedback via interviews rather than surveys.

**The Floor**

Cost-plus pricing is often derided as a weak pricing strategy, but it plays an essential role in setting the floor for a startup's pricing options. An accurate analysis of costs per unit plus a margin representing a minimally acceptable return on investment reveals a new product's lowest reasonable price level. If the market can't bear it, the startup must rethink the product's commercial viability.

Although the cost-plus model is well known, startups often struggle in two areas when they use it to analyze their costs. First, they do not account for all costs that should be allocated to products. There is a tendency to overlook research and development (R&D) expenses associated with a product category, including expenses for incomplete projects and goodwill linked to acquisitions that lead directly to new products. As a necessary part of any R&D program, these are legitimate costs to calculate. Second, overly optimistic market projections can create false estimates of costs, particularly fixed ones.

The range of pricing options is usually smallest for products that are similar to competitors. Startups need to assess their costs correctly and understand the assumptions underlying these calculations. A small error can permanently prevent products from becoming profitable.

# What are the types of pricing strategies?

There are a number of pricing strategies that a startup can use to sell its products. The strategy used at any specific time should depend on the startup's strategy and objectives. The typical types of pricing strategies include:

- **Penetration Pricing:** A low price is set by the startup to grow sales and market share. This may be done to establish position in a market with preexisting similar products available. Once an initial position is created by the startup, the prices can be raised.
- **Skimming Pricing:** The initial price is set high and is gradually reduced over time. This will allow the startup to introduce the product slowly to different layers of the market. Each part of the market may be willing to pay a different amount for the product. Consumer electronics often start at a very high price that is subsequently lowered with the lowest point reached right before a new model is launched.
- **Competition Pricing:** When trying to go head to head with competitors offering similar benefits, a company may decide to
  - Price higher to create a higher quality perception or target a niche market,
  - Price the same to show more benefits for the same price, or
  - Price lower to try to gain a wider customer base.
- **Product Line Pricing:** Different products in the same range may be set at different prices. Television sets are priced variously depending on the features of the television.
- **Bundle Pricing:** A group of products may be bundled together and sold at a reduced price. Retailers use this method through "buy one, get one free" offers.

- **Psychological Pricing:** A company will make small changes to prices to make a customer think the item is priced lower than it is. This is often observed when prices end in ninety-nine. For example, an item priced at 199 may be perceived as closer in price to 100 than 200. Or a monthly price may be charged for an annual subscription instead of the full annual price being charged initially.

- **Premium Pricing:** A high price is set to establish that the product is exclusive and of high quality. Exotic cars and luxury watches are examples of this type of pricing.

- **Optional Pricing:** A company may add optional extra items within the price to increase a product's attractiveness.

- **Cost Based Pricing:** A company may determine the exact cost of producing and selling a product, add a markup that may be desirable for profits, and price accordingly. This method may be used in a changing industry where even costs of production are unpredictable.

- **Cost Plus Pricing:** A percentage is added to the costs as a profit margin to determine the final price.

# How do you price a new product or service?

A startup's pricing strategy and methods change with circumstances and time. This is why there is no single best methodology. However, the following steps can act as a general guideline:

1. **Develop the Marketing Strategy:** A market analysis is a starting point for pricing decisions. Then, divide the market into segments with distinct requirements and needs. After this, determine which segment to target. The product and brand positioning is then based on these identified segments.

2. **Make Marketing Mix Decisions on 4Ps (Excluding Price):** Once the segments and positioning are in place, focus on the product, placement, and promotional decisions.

3. **Estimate the Demand Curve:** Another market analysis needs to be conducted at this point. In this one, there needs to be specific information gathered about how the price affects sales volume.

4. **Calculate Costs:** A company can now get an accurate assessment of the total fixed and variable costs associated with the product. These are a necessary inputs for pricing decisions, as the final price needs to at least cover these costs.

5. **Assess the Environment:** Another vital element that influences pricing is the environment. This demands an understanding of the competitor's strategies, their product, and its value, as well as an understanding of any industry or legal constraints.

6. **Set Pricing Objectives:** As detailed above, there are several objectives that a startup can have in terms of its pricing strategy. This is the point in the process that those objectives need to be discussed and agreed upon.

7. **Determine Price:** Using all of the information collected and analyzed until this point, a startup is now in a good position to set the best price for its products. A pricing method and structure can be formulated along with any possible sales promotions or discounts.

# What factors affect pricing?

There are several basic factors that affect pricing for almost all startups and large companies. These can be categorized as internal factors and external factors.

- **Internal Factors:** These are the elements that are under the control of the startup. However, it is vital to note that though they may be within the startup's domain of control, changing them may not be as easy as it seems. For example, production process changes may require significant cost, time, and process redesign. Internal factors include:
  - Fixed and variable costs
  - Company objectives and strategies
  - Market segments, targeting, and positioning decisions

- **External Factors:** Those factors that have a significant impact on pricing decisions, but are not completely controllable by the startup, are known as external factors. Since these are very important to the pricing decision, a company can exert control by conducting detailed analyses to understand in depth how these factors will have an impact. External factors may include
  - Competitors
  - Target market behavior and willingness to pay
  - Industry trends
  - Industry or legal constraints

# What pricing issues are difficult?

In business, there are often gray areas that might seem simple, but are difficult to address. Issues such as the minimum wage of a state, worker benefits required by law, and safe work environment policies are easy to understand. Alternatively, pricing strategies can be quite blurry and difficult to judge in terms of ethics. Though there are legal measures in place to prevent unethical pricing methods, there are many areas not controlled by laws that can nonetheless create negative situations for buyers and startups. For example, misleading promotional campaigns or the use of low quality materials when better is expected can lead to wrong buying decisions.

It is often impossible to prove that a misstep by a startup was deliberate or not. These gray areas can also be entered accidentally by a startup. Gray areas to be mindful of include

- **Price Fixing:** In a competitive market, prices are often lowered to the benefit of the consumer. If these competitors were to communicate and decide to sell at a common price, it would likely result in more expensive products for the user and more benefits for the companies. It is therefore a good idea for a startup to study the competition and the market, but not to enter non-compete agreements that harm the consumer.

- **Price Discrimination:** When the same product is sold at different prices to different sets of consumers, it is called price discrimination. This is a challenging category, as special offers for seniors and children are acceptable, while presenting only high cost options to higher-income consumers might not be well received.

- **Price Skimming:** When a product is priced high initially and then eventually sold at a lower price, it is called price skimming. The company aims to gather higher profits from premium users first and then slowly move down the chain to access all levels of consumer groups. Usually employed in the technology industry, if this technique is not managed well, it can create a negative impression in the consumer's mind. Eventually, customers may catch on to the pattern and stop buying until a lower price is introduced.

- **Opportunistic Pricing:** At times, the value attached to a product may be much higher than its cost. This allows a startup to charge a premium price for their products for a limited time period. The gray area here is whether the startup should follow this practice in all instances. If there is a shortage of a necessary good or a special situation such as a natural disaster, then this opportunistic pricing may be unethical and perhaps illegal. However, software and other select products that may be less expensive to produce, but offer great benefit might be able to charge higher prices with less criticism.. It is a good idea for a startup to assess whether its premium pricing policy limits a consumer's access to a necessary item such as food or medicine.

In summary, pricing plays a very important role in determining a product's perceived value, in building brands, and in ensuring long-term profits and sales for the startup. It is therefore important to give it due attention and allow in-depth analyses to become the basis of pricing decisions.

# 4.2 PLACEMENT

In the marketing mix, the process of moving products from the producer to the intended user is called placement. Placement involves the process and methods used to bring the product or service to the consumer. Placement will deal with how your product is bought and where it is bought. This movement can occur through a combination of intermediaries such as distributors, wholesalers, and retailers. In addition, a newer method is the internet, which itself is a marketplace now.

Through the use of the right placement, a startup can increase sales and maintain these over a longer period of time. In turn, this result can mean a greater share of the market and increased revenues and profits.

Correct placement is a vital activity that is focused on reaching the right target audience at the right time. It focuses on where the startup is located, where the target market is placed, how best to connect these two, how to store goods in the interim, and how to eventually transport them.

Multiple placements may also be beneficial for companies. For example, Dell is widely available today from its own website, to Amazon.com, and other retailers. This is a dramatic shift from Dell's first strategy of being exclusively available from the company itself via phone orders (in a time before the Internet was popularly available).

In this chapter, we will explore the fundamentals of placement, distribution channels and intermediaries, making channel decisions, managing distribution channels, and the impact of the marketing mix on placement. We will also examine Dell's strategy.

# Dell's Placement on Dell's Website

> ⌂ > For Home > Laptops & 2-in-1s > Inspiron Laptops & 2-in-1 PCs > Inspiron 13 5000 2-in-1 > Inspiron 13 5000 2-in-1

Intel® Core™ Processors
Compare

## Inspiron 13 5000 2-in-1

★★★★ 3.9 (3128)   Write a review   Ask a question

### Picture the possibilities.

13-inch 2-in-1 in a sleek and portable design with stunning sound and features like a backlit keyboard and infrared camera for facial recognition.

Starting at $699.99

Financing
As low as $21/mo.^ | Apply

[ Add to Cart ]

# Dell's Placement on Amazon's Website

INSPIRON LAPTOPS     INSPIRON ALL-IN-ONE     XPS     ALIENWARE     DELL GAMING     SMALL BUSINESS ▾     MONITORS ▾     ACCESSORIES

## Dell Inspiron 13 5000 2-in-1 - 13.3" FHD Touch - 8th Gen Intel i5-8250U - 8GB Memory - 256GB SSD - Intel UHD Graphics 620 - Theoretical Gray - i5379-5893GRY-PUS

★★★☆☆  40 customer reviews

- 8th Generation Intel Core i5-8250U Processor (6MB Cache, up to 3.4 GHz)
- 8GB 2400MHz DDR4 up to [16GB], (additional memory sold separately)

˅ Show more

$649$^{99}$ ✓prime

Ships from and sold by Amazon.com.

| ADD TO CART | SEE BUYING OPTIONS |

# What is a distribution channel?

A distribution channel can be defined as a spatial metaphor for the activities and processes required to move a product from the producer to the consumer. Also included in the channel are the intermediaries that are involved in this movement in any capacity. These intermediaries are third party companies that act as wholesalers, transporters, retailers, and warehousers.

There are four main types of distribution channels:

- **Direct:** The manufacturer directly provides the product to the consumer. In this instance, the company m own all elements of its distribution channel or sell through a specific retail location. Internet sales and one-on-one meetings are also ways to sell directly to the consumer. One benefit of this method is that the company has complete control over the product, its image at all stages, and the user experience.

- **Indirect:** A company will use an intermediary to sell a product to the consumer. The company may sell to a wholesaler who further distributes to retail outlets. This may raise product costs since each intermediary will get a percentage of the profits. This channel may become necessary for large producers who sell through hundreds of small retailers.

- **Dual Distribution:** A company may use a combination of direct and indirect selling. The product may be sold directly to a consumer in some cases, while in other cases it may be sold through intermediaries. This type of channel may help reach more consumers, but there may be the danger of channel conflict. The user experience may vary, and an inconsistent image for the product and a related service may begin to take hold.

- **Reverse Channels:** The last, most non-traditional channel allows for the consumer to send a product to the producer. This reverse flow is what distinguishes this method from the others. An example of this is when a consumer recycles and makes money from this activity.

# What is an intermediary?

Intermediaries are those who play a crucial role in the distribution process. They facilitate the distribution process through their experience and expertise.

There are four main types of intermediaries:

- **Agents:** The agent is an independent entity who acts as an extension of the producer by representing the company to the user. An agent never actually gains ownership of the product and usually make money from commissions and fees paid for their services.
- **Wholesalers:** Wholesalers are also independent entities. But they actually purchase goods from a producer in bulk and store them in warehouses. These goods are then resold in smaller amounts at a profit. Wholesalers seldom sell directly to an end user. Their customers are usually another intermediary such as a retailer.
- **Distributors:** Similar to wholesalers, distributors differ from them in in that wholesalers generally carry a variety of competition brands and product types, whereas a distributor will only carry products from a single brand or company. A distributor may have a close relationship with the producer.
- **Retailers:** Wholesalers and distributors will sell the products that they have acquired to the retailer at a profit. Retailers will then stock the goods and sell them to the ultimate end user at a profit.

# Why are distribution channels important?

It may seem simpler and smarter for a startup to directly distribute its own products without the help of a channel and intermediaries. This is especially true because the internet allows sellers and buyers to interact in real time. In practice, it may not make business sense for a startup to set up its own distribution operation. Large scale producers of consumer goods, for example, need to stock items of basic necessity such as soap, toilet paper, and toothpaste in as many small and large stores in as many locations as possible. These locations may be as close together as two on the same street. They may also be sold at remote rural convenience stores, rest stops, and gasoline stations. It would be counterproductive and costly for a startup to attempt to achieve this kind of dispersion without a detailed distribution channel.

Even in cases where a startup does sell directly, there remain activities that are performed by an outside company. A laptop may be sold from a company website to a consumer directly, but it will be sent out using an existing courier service. This is why, in one form or another, many producers rely on a distribution channel.

# How do you make channel decisions?

To determine the best distribution channel to use, a startup needs to:

- Analyze the customer and understand his or her needs,
- Discuss and finalize channel objectives, and
- Work out distribution tasks and processes.

Key questions to ask in these three areas include

- Where do customers typically attempt to purchase the product?
- If the item is sold at a physical store, is it a supermarket or a specialist store? Is it an online store or a catalogue?
- What level of access is available to the candidate distribution channels?
- What are competitors doing? Are they successful? What are best practices in channel decisions?

A startup may need to use different strategies for different types of products. Three main strategies that can be used are

- **Intensive Distribution:** This strategy may be used to distribute low-priced products that may be impulse purchases. Items are stocked at a large number of retailers as is the case with mints, gum, or candy, as well as basic supplies and necessities.
- **Selective Distribution:** In this strategy, a product may be sold at a select number or outlets. These may include items such as computers or appliances that are costly, but need to be widely available to allow consumers to compare choices.
- **Exclusive Distribution:** A higher priced item may be sold at a single outlet. This is exclusive distribution. New automobiles may be an example of this type of strategy.

# What are the benefits of distribution channels?

While making channel decisions, a startup may need to weigh the benefits of a partner with the associated costs, including:

- **Specialists:** Since intermediaries are experts at what they do, they can perform the task better and more cost effectively than a startup itself.

- **Quick Exchange Time:** Being specialists and using established processes, intermediaries are able to ensure deliveries faster and on time.

- **Variety for the Consumers:** By selling through retailers, consumers are able to choose between varieties of products without having to visit multiple stores belonging to each individual producer.

- **Small Quantities:** Intermediaries allow the cost of transportation to be divided, and this situation will, in turn, allow consumers to buy small quantities of a product rather than having to make bulk purchases. This is possible when a wholesaler buys in bulk, stores the product in a warehouse, and then provides the product to retailers located close by at lower transportation costs.

- **Sales Creation:** Since retailers and wholesalers have their own stakes in the product, they may have their own advertising or promotion efforts that help generate sales.

- **Payment Options:** Retailers may create payment plans and options for customers, thus allowing for easier purchasing.

- **Information:** The distribution channel can provide valuable information on the product and its acceptability, allowing product development as well as an idea of emerging consumer trends and behaviors.

What are the consequences of distribution channels?

With the benefits of distribution channels in mind, there are consequences that a startup may incur when making channel decisions such as the following:

- **Lost Revenue:** Because intermediaries need to be either paid for their services or allowed to resell at a higher price, the startup may lose out on revenue. Pricing needs to stay consistent, so the startup will have to reduce its profit margin to give a share to the intermediary.

- **Lost Communication Control:** Along with revenue, the message being received by the consumer is also in the hands of the intermediary. There is a danger of the intermediary communicating inaccurate information to the customer regarding product features and benefits, and this can lead to consumer dissatisfaction.

- **Lost Product Importance:** When a product is handed over to an intermediary, how much importance is accorded to it is now out of the startup's hand. The intermediary may have incentives to push another product first at the expense of yours.

## What are the keys to managing distribution channels?

Channel management is an essential activity for startups. Intermediaries need to be kept motivated and offered incentives to ensure timely and efficient delivery of products and services. Clear messages regarding products and their functionalities need to be passed on to attempt to keep clear communication regarding a product or brand all the way to the end user.

As is the case when a customer base is segmented and addressed according to their specific needs and requirements, distribution channels can also be segmented. Not all intermediaries or the markets they serve will be similar. There may be a need to foster stronger relationships with a retailer that sells in a knowledgeable and discerning market with a high amount of competition. Similarly, if a product is expensive and highly specialized, a retailer may need to be trained and given the relevant information.

A startup can achieve one of more of the following benefits through proper channel segmentation:

- **Product Management:** Relevant products can be provided to the right channel, a process which can help reduce the cost of irrelevant inventory as well as unnecessary logistical arrangements.
- **Price Management:** Local price differentiation may be possible.
- **Promotion Management:** Targeted and relevant promotional activities may be improved with clear and consistent marketing messages.
- **Efficiency in Operations:** Time and resource wastage in the channel can be reduced. The development needs of every channel segment can be addressed separately, in a more targeted manner.

# What is the impact of the marketing mix on placement?

No element of the marketing mix works best in isolation. Information from each of them acts as input to the others. This is why when shaping a distribution strategy, input needs to be taken from all other elements of the marketing mix, and any considerations need to be addressed or incorporated. Product, price, and promotion may have the following impacts on the distribution strategy:

- **Impact of Product Issues:** The type of product being manufactured is often the deciding factor in distribution decisions. A delicate or perishable product will need special arrangements, while sturdy or durable products will not require such delicate handling.

- **Impact of Pricing Issues**: An assessment of the right price for a product is made by the startup team. This is the price at which the customer will be willing to make the purchase. This price will often help decide the type of distribution channel. If this price does not allow a high margin, then a company may choose to use fewer intermediaries in its channel to ensure that everyone gets her share at a reasonable cost to the manufacturer.

- **Impact of Promotion Issues:** The nature of the product also has an impact on the type of promotions required to sell it. These promotion decisions will, in turn, directly affect the distribution decisions. Disposable goods or those of everyday use do not require too many special channels. If the product or service is complex to use or understand, a specialist channel may be needed.

## Case Study: Direct Selling at Dell

Dell was founded by a college freshman, Michael Dell. By 1985, the company had developed its unique strategy of offering made to order computers. Sales went from $6 million in 1984 to $70 million in 1985. In another five years, the sales jumped to $500 million, and by the end of 2000, they had crossed $25 billion.

A superior supply chain and innovative manufacturing played important roles in this phenomenal success. Another important contributing factor was the unique distribution strategy employed by the company. Identifying and capitalizing on an emerging market trend, Dell eliminated intermediaries and/or retailers from their distribution channel. This was done after studying and analyzing the personal computer value chain.

Dell became a strong direct seller by using mail-order systems before the spread of the Internet. After the Internet became more mainstream, it established an online sales platform. Early in the Internet era, Dell began providing order status reports and technical support to their customers online. Online sales reached $4 million a day in 1997.

While competitors sold pre-configured and assembled PCs in retail stores, Dell offered a new experience to customers by providing them with the ability to pick desirable features and lower the price that they paid for these features. This was possible because Dell did not have to bear the costs of the intermediary.

Another useful aspect of this model was the information available regarding customers and their needs and requirements. This helped the company predict market trends and segment its market. This segmentation helped product development efforts and improved the company's understanding of what creates value for each segment.

Through careful analysis of the target market, a study of available channel options, and effective use of a novel idea, Dell established itself in the market, and the company continues to be a market leader today.

# 4.3 PROMOTION

The promotion elements of the marketing mix includes all of the activities that involve communicating with the customer about the product and its benefits and features. This includes raising awareness of the product through different media to increase sales, as well as to create and foster brand loyalty.

Information provided to the prospective customer helps them to make purchasing decisions regarding the product. Often, there is substantial cost associated with promotional activities. But since the result is often an increase in sales or customer loyalty, there is thought to be long-term return on this investment. The typical goals of a startup's promotional activities include an increase in sales, acceptance of new products, improved brand equity, an ability to address competitor actions, and the process of rebranding.

Promotion is the communication aspect of the marketing mix. It is creating a channel for conversation with the targeted customer. Through promotion, startups aim to attract the customer's attention and give them enough information about the product to foster enough interest to motivate the customer to make a purchase.

Promotional activities start with developing an understanding of the dynamics of the target audience and deciding which modes of promotion are best. Once the channel is decided, information from other elements of the marketing mix is incorporated to ensure that the message sent corresponds to the actual product features, benefits, and user experience. None of the elements of the marketing mix work in isolation. Instead, a unified body of information acts as the source for all of the activities in that mix.

To appreciate how innovative promotions vary widely in their products and services promoted, and the diversity of how promotions are presented to prospective customers, investigate Fast Company's list of The Word's Most Innovative Companies in Marketing and Advertising.[3]

---

[3] Fast Company (2018). The Word's Most Innovative Companies in Marketing and Advertising. https://www.fastcompany.com/most-innovative-companies/2018/sectors/marketing-and-advertising

# The Word's Most Innovative Companies in Marketing and Advertising in 2018

## 1 Wieden+Kennedy

For redefining the viral stunt for Nike, the spokescharacter for KFC, and the agency itself

## 2 Adidas

For challenging itself - and customers - with the All Day lifestyle app

## 3 Yeti

For making branded content films that give the rough outdoors heart and soul

## 4 Cycle Media

For building the holding company for the 21st century

## 5 Forsman & Bodenfors

For letting us rent Sweden on Airbnb and thinking inside the box for Uber

## 6 3AM

For upping the ambition on movie marketing with its Blade Runner 2049 prequel

## 7 BBDO

For hacking Instagram stories for Bacardi to create a DJ app

## 8 Frito-Lay

For sprinkling magic dust on Cheetos with a museum and a pop-up restaurant

## 9 Red Antler

For crafting identities for breakthrough brands like Crooked Media and Brandless

## 10 Collectively

For pairing 75 brands with 1,725 influencers to create 1.2 billion impressions

In this chapter, we will explore the role of promotion in the marketing mix, the objectives of promotional activities, major targets of promotional activities, the promotional mix, types of promotional strategies, managing promotion through the product life cycle, and an example of the promotion mix in action.

# What are the objectives of promotion?

Different startups may have different expectations for their promotional activities. These expectations are developed into objectives which then shape the selection and execution of the promotional activities. Typical objectives of promotion for a startup may include:

- **Building Awareness:** In the beginning, startups typically need to create an identity within the market. This applies to a new company, a new brand, or a new product. Often, this identity will also be important in times of rebranding or building up a failing product. The aim then is to select those promotional activities that help inform the customer about the company, the brand, and/or the product.

- **Creating Interest:** If the customer is already aware of the product or has been made aware through other activities, it becomes necessary to move them along to actual purchasing behavior. The aim is to identify a need that the product fulfills and make sure that the customer recognizes this need as unfulfilled for them.

- **Providing Information:** A startup may need to provide necessary information regarding the product, its benefits, features, or usage to the customer. This may be the case if a new product is introduced into the market. Unique features or benefits may need to be explained. In other cases, a new feature on an existing product may need to be highlighted. In some cases, such as in instances when environmental impact or health scares may be in play, information about a change in business practices and company policy may need to be communicated.

- **Stimulating Demand:** A startup may seek to start or enhance its sales through promotion. At the start of the company, initial sales are the priority. Later, if sales have been lower than usual, then the aim may be to get them back up to target level by re-engaging old customers and encouraging new ones to try a product. In other instances, the aim may be to increase sales further at certain times of the year such as near a major holiday. Free demonstrations or special deals may be used to reach these ends.

- **Differentiating the Product:** In situations in which there are many competitors in the market, a startup may seek to use promotional activities to differentiate its product from others in the market and make it stand out from the crowd. The focus remains on those features, functionalities, or benefits that may not be offered by a competitor or may not be offered well.

- **Reinforcing the Brand:** One basic aim of a promotional activity may be to further strengthen the brand and its place in the market. This helps turn a first time purchaser into a lifetime purchaser. This can also create advocates for the product from within the customer base.

# Who are the audiences for promotional activities?

Every promotional activity should be designed with a specific objective and target audience in mind. The activity is therefore created using messages, cues, and information to which customers will respond. Realistically, the major portion of any promotional budget is aimed at this specific targeted audience. However, there may be important fringe groups who may have an influence over the intended target or stake in the product. These fringe groups may include:

- **Customers:** These are the current customers of the product as well as former customers and any potential new customers. The activity is created for these people specifically.

- **Influencers:** People or organizations that may have their own sphere of influence over the target audience make up this category. If a positive impact is made on these people, they may then use this influence to encourage sales. Members of the media, opinion leaders, trade associations, and special interest groups are examples of influencers.

- **Distribution Channel Members:** The product is handled and provided to the customer through this channel making them an important category of targets. A retailer may choose to display a certain product in a more prominent position than the others if she believes in the product and its benefits.

- **Other Companies:** Communicating with other companies may open up opportunities to collaborate.

# What is the promotional mix?

There is a tendency to narrow down the focus of promotional activities to advertising only. However, there are a number of ways to approach the audience with information about the product. Increasingly, businesses feel the need to use both unidirectional and bidirectional means of communication to reach the customer.

Through the promotional mix, a startup aims to fulfill two basic objectives: one is to make the customer aware that the company, brand, and product exist; the other is to persuade customers to actually pick this product over all others and continue to buy it.

There are five methods that make up a promotional mix. A startup may choose to use one or more of these in harmony to ensure that a clear, effective, and direct message reaches the customer. The selection of the portfolio of activities may depend on the startup's marketing and sales strategies, as well as budget allocations.

These five methods of the promotional mix are:

- **Advertising:** This mode of promotion is usually monetary, with little or no personal message. Mass media such as television, radio, newspapers, and magazines are most often the carriers of these messages. Apart from these, billboards, posters, web pages, brochures, and direct mail also fall within this category. While this method has traditionally been one-sided, online advertising may allow for interactive engagement with prospective customers.

- **Public Relations & Sponsorship:** Public relations (PR) or publicity departments try to increase positive mention of the company, brand, or product in influential media outlets. These could include newspapers, magazines, talk shows, and new media such as social networks and blogs. This could also mean allowing super users, or influencers, to test the product and speak positively about it to their peers. This type of advertisement may or may not be paid. For example, sponsoring a major event and increasing brand visibility is a paid action. Sending free samples to a blogger then depends on his discretion and opinion and is not usually swayed by payment.

- **Personal Selling:** Opposite of one-directional promotional methods, direct selling connects company representatives with the consumer. These interactions can be in person, over the phone, over email, or through chat. This personal contact aims to create a personal relationship between the client and the company, brand, or product.

- **Direct Marketing:** This channel targets specific influential potential customers through telemarketing, customized letters, emails, and text messages.

- **Sales Promotions:** These are usually short-term strategic activities which aim to encourage a surge in sales. These could be "buy one, get one free" options, seasonal discounts, contests, samples or special coupons with expiration dates.

Whenever a startup sets out to design its promotional mix, it needs to consider the following points:

- **Stage in the Product Life Cycle:** During the beginning of the life cycle, there may need to be more aggressive and informational advertising emphasis, while a slowdown in promotions is possible during the later stages.

- **Nature of the Product:** If a product is not new in its usage or function, there may be less need for information and more focus on brand equity creation, as well as on the emotional aspects of the product.

- **The Allocated and Available Budget:** A total budget is set for promotional activities, and these activities then need to be designed and executed within the allotted budget.

- **Cultural Sensitivity:** If a product is to be launched in a new international market or translated across markets, it becomes imperative to take into consideration local affiliations and sensitivities. These include cultural, religious, and regional values. Often, these issues can even present themselves within one country.

- **Target Market Composition:** The people who make up the target market need to be considered before committing to a promotional mix. If a market is not tech savvy, then more traditional means may need to be employed. Conversely, an internet generation used to instant gratification may need to be provided more focused and targeted messages.

- **Competitor Actions:** The methods a competitor uses need to be taken into account as well. There may not be a need to spend money on a radical advertising method if a customer is using rudimentary methods.

# What are the typical types of promotional strategies?

A startup can use different strategies to promote its products. These can be broadly categorized as push and pull strategies. The strategies differ in how the customer is approached.

- **Push Strategies:** As the name indicates, this is when the product is taken to the customer by the startup. This is typically used when the product is an impulse purchase, or if the company has an established relationship with the customer base. Startups may sell directly from their showrooms or at trade shows. Essentially, there is less need to create an advertising buzz and more focus on making the product readily available at retail outlets and showrooms. Push marketing will often focus primarily on short term sales.

- **Pull Strategies:** In the opposite approach, there is an attempt to pull customers towards the brand or product. Through mass media campaigns to sales promotions and personal references, a company attempts to create brand loyalty and attractiveness. Pull strategies may attempt to focus primarily first on long-term brand loyalty, then high sales in the short term. A lot of media hype and mass campaigns are required to create sufficient interest in the product and encourage customers to seek out the product on their own.

Most companies will use a mix of these two strategies at different points in time.

# How do you manage promotions through the product life cycle?

The different stages of the product life cycle require different types of promotional activities and strategies. This will help prolong the life of the product. Each of these product life cycles stages will be examined in turn.

1. **Introduction:** At this stage, major promotional campaigns and activities will be designed and executed. A comprehensive promotional mix will be designed, fully integrated the rest of the marketing mix. The aim here is to provide detailed information about the product, its features and benefits. Special offers and sales promotions may also be used to attract customers, while in select markets, push strategies may be simultaneously employed.

2. **Growth:** Once the product is established and accepted, there will be a shift in strategy from information to the more emotional aspects of sales. The aim is to increase brand awareness, create strong brand equity, and foster long-term customer loyalty.

3. **Maturity:** By now the market may have matured, and there may be stiff competition and similar products available. Promotional activities will now turn more persuasive. There may be an attempt to create product differentiation by highlighting specific benefits and features that fulfill needs and wants.

4. **Decline:** At this point, promotional activities may wind down to the occasional reminder that the product exists in an attempt to forestall the product's eventual decline.

# Case Study: Promotions at Skoda

Skoda is one of the world's oldest automobile manufacturers, created over 120 years ago in the Czech Republic. Skoda has experienced high variances in its popularity as a brand over the course of its long history. At its lowest point, it was perceived as an outdated brand with obsolete manufacturing techniques. Through a combination of new techniques, a new partner, and an effective PR strategy, the brand was turned around and a new image created.

## Public Relations at Skoda

There is no short term solution to change long-held perceptions. If there is to be a long term change in perception, it needs to be achieved through sustained and consistent actions over a significant period of time. PR activities are an example of such a solution in which positive messages are sent through different media to the public, eventually establishing a positive reputation over time.

## The Image Problem

Skoda needed an image makeover in the United Kingdom where it was not widely viewed as a desirable brand. In 1991, the brand was purchased by Volkswagen. This enabled the company to redesign its manufacturing process and bring about product quality and positive brand image, one on par with competitors in the United Kingdom and eventually the world.

Despite this shift, customer perception remained negative, an unfortunate carryover from the past. Products were updated, and the brand was able to offer more to the consumer. The next challenge was to educate the audience on these changes and bring about a change in perception.

## The Challenge

The attempt to change opinion was divided into two challenges: the first was to move negative perceptions to neutral, and the second was to move neutral perceptions to positive. An integrated press and PR plan was devised and launched to address the first challenge and explain the changed company and product to the audience. Factory visits, meetings, and interviews with designers and engineers, motor shows, sponsorships, displays at public arenas, and well-planned advertisement campaigns were part of this strategy. These efforts helped reduce the strong negative image and create the basis for further shift towards a positive image.

In attempting to address the second challenge, the company needed to encourage consumers to think about buying the product. This is not typically possible only through advertising. There needs to be a focus on building up the brand and communicating what it stands for. This was done by emphasizing Skoda's brand values through cars that were practical, reliable, functional, and robust. This was also reiterated through a focus on quality and value for money.

## The Result

Through this PR effort, and subsequent important brand launches, the modern Skoda brand was established, thus allowing the company to step successfully into the future.

# Worksheet for
## The Startup Analysis Canvas Project
## Phase 3 – Market Strategy

Each of the phases build on one another, as they're all connected to the same new product or service idea. In this phase, you will craft the Market Strategy for your new startup company.

## 1. Product

The Lean Product Process is an iterative, easy-to-follow process based on the Product-Market Fit Pyramid. This process guides you sequentially through each layer of the pyramid from the bottom to the top. The process helps you articulate, test, and revise your key hypotheses so that you can improve your product-market fit. Be sure to integrate your team's prior work on this topic from earlier submissions.

- Who is your target customer?
- What are the underserved needs of this target customer?
- What is your value proposition?
- What is your MVP feature set?
- What is your prototype?
  - If your idea is an app or website, include a wireframe generated from Balsamiq or a comparable tool.
  - If your idea is a product, include a sketch, diagram, or rendering of the product.
  - If your idea is a service, include a flowchart of how the service works.

## 2. Price

- What is the market size of the target market that you've selected?
    - Be sure to quantify this in terms of users and their annual spending on the product or service that you will provide.
    - Include at least three references to support your market-size assessment.
- What are your costs to create, develop, and deliver the product or service?
- What are pricing strategies of your direct and indirect competitors?
- What is your pricing strategy for your product or service?
    - Explain why this is the best strategy.

## 3. Placement

- What types of Distribution Channels will you use? Please discuss which of the following four channels you will use and why.
    - Direct: In this channel, the manufacturer directly provides the product to the consumer. In this instance, the business may own all elements of its distribution channel or sell through a specific retail location. Internet sales and one-on-one meetings are also ways to sell directly to the consumer. One benefit of this method is that the company has complete control over the product, its image at all stages, and the user experience.
    - Indirect: In this channel, a company will use an intermediary to sell a product to the consumer. The company may sell to a wholesaler who further distributes to retail outlets. This may raise product costs since each intermediary will get its own percentage of the profits. This channel may become necessary for large producers who sell through hundreds

of small retailers.

- o Dual Distribution: In this type of channel, a company may use a combination of direct and indirect sales. The product may be sold directly to a consumer, while in other cases it may be sold through intermediaries. This type of channel may help a business reach more consumers, but there may be the danger of channel conflict. The user experience may vary, and an inconsistent image for the product and a related service may begin to take hold.

- o Reverse Channels: The last, most non-traditional channel allows for the consumer to send a product to the producer. This reverse flow is what distinguishes this method from the others. An example of this is when a consumer recycles and makes money from this activity.

- What types of intermediaries will you use? Please discuss which of the below four intermediaries you will use and why.

- o Agents: The agent is an independent entity who acts as an extension of the producer by representing her to the user. An agent never actually gains ownership of the product and usually makes money from commissions and fees paid for their services.

- o Wholesalers: Wholesalers are also independent entities. But they actually purchase goods from a producer in bulk and store them in warehouses. These goods are then resold in smaller amounts at a profit. Wholesalers seldom sell directly to an end user. Their customers are usually another intermediary such as a retailer.

- o Distributors: Similar to wholesalers, distributors differ in one regard: a wholesaler will generally carry a variety of competition brands and product types, whereas a distributor will only carry products from a single brand or company. A distributor may have a close relationship with the producer.

- o Retailers: Wholesalers and distributors will sell the products that they have acquired to the retailer at a profit. Retailers will then stock the goods and sell them to the ultimate end user at a profit.

## 4. Promotion

- What types of advertising will you use for your product or service in year one?
    - o  What is the cost of doing so?
    - o  Be sure to include a specific dollar value.
- What types of public relations and sponsorships will you employ for your product or service in year one?
    - o  What is the cost of doing so?
    - o  Be sure to include a specific dollar value.
- Will you use personal selling as part of your promotional strategy?
    - o  Why or why not?
- Will you use direct marketing as part of your promotional strategy?
    - o  Why or why not?
- Will you use sales promotions as part of your promotional strategy?
    - o  Why or why not?

# 5.0 FINANCIAL STRATEGY

The fourth and final area of the Startup Analysis Canvas is financial strategy. This includes the revenue model, cost model, sales model, and funding model.

## The Startup Analysis Canvas - Focus on Financial Strategy

| 1 Value Proposition | | 2 Team Strategy | |
|---|---|---|---|
| | Problem | | Founders |
| | Competition | | Advisers |
| | Product-Market Fit | | Partners |

| 3 Market Strategy | | 4 Financial Strategy | |
|---|---|---|---|
| | Price | | Revenue Model |
| | Placement | | Cost Model |
| | Promotion | | Sales Model |
| | | | Funding Model |

Before beginning our exploration of the revenue model, we will explore the funding dilemma and how startup valuation works.

## The Funding Dilemma

In the two years after Lew Cirne founded Wily Technology in 1997, he assembled an experienced executive team, hired fifty employees, and raised two rounds of venture capital funding. To raise funding, he had to relinquish three of the five board seats to his investors, who promptly decided that Cirne should be replaced by a CEO with a stronger business background. CA Technologies, one of the world's largest software development companies, eventually bought the firm for $375 million. While this was viewed as a successful outcome for Wily, the founder was still chagrined about the early decisions he made that led to his ouster.

Whether in Silicon Valley or any of the other startup hubs around the world, Cirne's dilemma is all too familiar. To grow their firms, founders often need financing, skilled employees, and the kind of "social buzz" that makes investors reach for their checkbooks. But the more investors or key hires who come aboard to provide much-needed resources, the more control the company founder must surrender. Founders often face a trade-off between retaining control and increasing the value of a young firm.

As detailed in the 2016 article titled "The throne vs. the kingdom: Founder control and value creation in startups," Noam Wasserman studied the competing interests of startup funding versus founder control.[4] Wasserman studies over six thousand high-potential U.S.-based startups that launched between 2005 and 2012. He found that how a founder navigates this early-stage founder's dilemma has a profound impact on the firm's long-term value. The more power retained by founders, Wasserman discovered, the less valuable their companies become.

---

[4] Wasserman, N. (2015). The throne vs. the kingdom: Founder control and value creation in startups. *Strategic Management Journal, 38* (2), 255-277.

Based on this study, for every additional position of power a founder occupies (being both CEO and chairman, for example, as opposed to controlling just one of those roles), the company's value decreased by between 17.1% and 22%. The author also found that startups whose founders retained an additional level of power saw a 35.8% to 51.4% decrease in the amount of financing they raised, depending on which variables he used to measure a founder's control.

But this trade-off effect only becomes evident after three years, at that delicate stage in which founders' technical expertise or visionary outlook typically become less crucial to growth than the resources a firm has attracted.

Not only do these findings have major implications for how entrepreneurs should set up and structure their firms, but they also serve as lessons for the people who want to work at or invest in a promising startup. Investors who seek to maximize their returns and potential hires who want to be part of a fast-growing enterprise should do their due diligence on founders to understand their motivations and determine whether they'll be willing to cede power at the appropriate time.

Wasserman also discovered a potential downside to ushering founders out of the door: heightened risk. Bringing venture capital into the picture can ratchet up the pressure to "swing for the fences." And replacing a charismatic or creative founding CEO can give investors pause. Stakeholders and employees looking for security rather than growth spurts should seek out founders who refuse to step down and instead, in the words of Cirne, remain the "parent of [their babies]."

# How Startup Valuation Works

What is your startup company worth? That is the question you will be asking yourself when you are deciding to share equity with co-founders, early employees, and investors. Understanding the value of your company in the earliest stages of life is a tremendous challenge.

## Why does startup valuation matter?

Valuation matters to entrepreneurs because it determines the share of the company they exchange for money from an investor. At the earliest stage of the company, the economic worth of the startup is close to zero since minimal proof of the company's value exists, with few if any customers and revenues. However, the valuation has to be a lot higher than zero. Why? If you are seeking a seed investment of $100,000 in exchange for ten percent of your company, your pre-money valuation will be $1,000,000. Simply divide $100,000 by .10. This however, does not mean that your company is necessarily worth $1,000,000 now. You probably could not sell the company for that amount of money at that time. Valuation at the early stages is about the growth potential, as opposed to the present economic value.

## How do you calculate your valuation at the early stages?

At the inception of your startup, recognize that while you may see enormous opportunity and value in your idea, there are significant unknowns on how effective the idea is and whether it will translate into a successful, highly profitable company. The valuation of your startup is influenced by your ideas and plans, as well as the risks and costs associated with navigating these unknown elements of the startup journey.

1. The first step is to calculate how much money you need to grow to a point where you will show significant traction and raise the next round of investment. This may be $100,000, to support the company for eighteen months. An investor typically does not have an incentive to negotiate you down from this number. Why? Because you should be able to explain why this is the minimum amount you need to grow to the next stage by showing an itemized lists of projected expenses, and revenues (if any). If you are not able to sustain the company via your own revenues and funding from founders, you need the investor's money to grow the business. Without this investment, you will not grow, and that is not in the investor's interest.

2. Once the amount of the investment is established, determine how much of the company that the founders and owners of the company are willing to sell to the investor in exchange for funding. Anything more than fifty percent will leave you, the founder, with little incentive to work hard. Also, it can't be forty percent because that will leave very little equity for investors in your next round of funding. Perhaps ten to twenty percent equity would be reasonable if this $100,000 is vital to grow the company. The exact percentage is a negotiation between the founders and the investors. This is influenced by the number of investors interested in investing in the company, which can result in investors competing by lowering the percentage of ownership that they require for the $100,000.

3. Assume the $100,000 is set and that ten percent equity is also set. That determines the pre-money valuation at $1,000,000, by dividing $100,000 by .10.

# How do you determine valuation?

## *Seed Stage*

Early-stage valuation is commonly described as "an art rather than a science." For our purposes, we will focus on the science side and integrate math to help assess the factors that influence startup valuation.

- **Traction** - Of all things that you can show an investor, traction is the number one thing that will convince them to invest. Companies need customers, and if investors see early evidence of customers, this helps answer the question of your market viability. Do customers care about your solution?. While there is not a universally accepted minimum for the number of customers that will convince investors of your worth and promise, think thousands (for a hardware product) or tens of thousands (for an app or software) instead of only a small group of friends and family.

- **Reputation** - Entrepreneurs who are well-known and/or have prior successful sales of their companies, called exits, tend to get higher valuations. If you lack reputation as a first-time entrepreneur, consider the role that your co-founders, early executive hires, and/or board of advisers can play enhancing the reputation of your startup and raising your valuation.

- **Revenues** - Revenues are value for all startups, particularly for startups serving business customers (B2B). Revenues make the startup easier to value because they can be used as multipliers in comparison to other startups that have raised funding. For example, if another company in your industry raised $1 million with revenues of $200,000 for the prior twelve months, their valuation was five times the revenues ($1 million / $200,000 = 5). So if you generated $100,000, five times this is $500,000, which would be your valuation.

- **Hotness of Industry** - If you are in a popular industry with investors, they may pay a premium.

Do you need a high valuation? Not necessarily. When you get a high valuation for your seed round, for the next round you need a higher valuation. That means you need to grow a lot between the two rounds. A rule a thumb would be that within eighteen months, you need to show that you grew ten times. If you don't, you either raise a "down round" if someone wants to fund a slow-growth business or you run out of cash.

There are two popular strategies used in seed-stage funding:

- **Go big or go home**: Raise as much as possible at the highest valuation possible and spend all of the money fast to grow as fast as possible. If this works, you can hope to get a much higher valuation in the next round, so high in fact that your seed round can pay for itself.
- **Raise as you go**: Raise only that which you absolutely need. Spend as little as possible. Aim for a steady growth rate. There is nothing wrong with steadily growing your startup and your valuation rising steadily as a consequence. It might not get you in the news, but you will raise your next round.

## Series A

In this stage, the focus is growth. How much have you grown in the last twelve to eighteen months? Growth means traction. It could also mean revenue. Usually, revenue does not grow if the user base does not grow ( since there is only so much you can charge your existing customers before you hit the limit).

Investors at this stage determine valuation using the multiple method, also called the comparable method, as described by Fred Wilson. As previously discussed, the idea is that there are companies out there similar enough to yours. Since at this stage you already have a revenue stream, to get your valuation, all you will need to do is find out how many times valuation is bigger than revenue – or in other words, what the multiple is. That multiple can be gleaned from these comparable companies. Once the multiple is determined, multiply your revenue by it, producing your valuation.

It is important to understand what the investor is thinking at every step.

- Investors are focused on making their profits at your exit, which is when you sell part of the company in an initial public offering (IPO) or when you are acquired or merge with another company.
- Next, they will think about how much money that it will take you to grow the company to the point that someone will buy it. What are your total expenses incurred to reach an exit, how much of this value can you cover via your revenues, and what's the remainder (which is your funding requirement)?
- The investor will figure out what percentage they desire to own. For the amount of money needed from them and in consideration of other current and future investors in your company, how much equity do they require given the amount of money that you need and the potential of your company?

# 5.1 REVENUE MODEL

In this chapter, we explore what revenue streams represent for you. We will discuss revenue streams, developing your revenue model, types of revenue streams, ways to generate revenue streams, key revenue model questions, and a case study.

## What are revenue streams?

If customers are the heart of the business, revenues are the blood that keeps the business alive. Startups must evaluate the value of the solutions that they provide to each customer segment. An accurate evaluation of this value can result in significant revenue streams being gained from the customer segment(s).

It isn't enough for "keep the customers happy" to serve as your business mandate. Businesses that solely focus on their customer's satisfaction are operating incomplete business models, ones in which revenue streams are often mismanaged.

Revenue streams need to be as clearly defined as possible. Hence, it is not enough to list the sources for your various revenue streams, but equally important to specify their pricing and projected life cycles. The reason for listing these details is to evaluate whether it is profitable for your business even to opt for a specific revenue stream or not. If the cost of designing, producing, and delivering a product or service is more than what the customer is willing to pay for it or greater than the revenues the product generates before its life cycle ends, then it does not make business sense to proceed with the product.

Many businesses hesitate to conduct a full analysis of their revenue streams because they feel unable to price it correctly without creating a complete prototype of the solution. As discussed in our pricing chapter, one valuable way to begin pricing a product or service is to understand how big a role the problem plays in the customer's life, and what he is willing to pay to solve the problem.

# Developing Your Revenue Model

The most important aspect of understanding the revenue streams of your business is the use of forecasting. This is an exercise carried out throughout the life of your business because as the business climate and industry evolve, so do your forecasts. Typically, there are two types of forecasts being carried out by businesses: top down and bottom up. Listed below are the most important factors to consider when deciding on the revenue model your startup will follow.

## Choose the Closest Fit

Select a revenue model that is the closest fit to your startup and its context. Your revenue model should essentially help set the direction of your development efforts. If your startup is characterized by a heavy presence of software developers or engineers, it may be prudent to invest in a technology model in which research and development take a large share of the organizational effort and focus.

## Magnify Your Value

The revenue model you pick must magnify the value that your startup has to offer. Your revenue model should highlight what sets your organization apart and how you are able to uniquely provide value to customers.

## Attract the Right Investors

The revenue model you select is also key to attracting the right kind of investors to your startup. When you pick development areas, it helps to know which of these areas are close to your target investors' interests and develop pitches around these areas. This choice helps to cement the legitimacy of your business in the investors' eyes. Fundamental to being successful in finding a good potential investor is to ensure that the investor takes a holistic view of your startup and is in it for the long haul as opposed to the myopic investor seeking a quick return on his investment.

## Focus on the First 1 to 2 Years

It is important to understand the long-term revenue potential for your startup. However, any predictions that go beyond one or two years are unrealistic and represent data that is not dependable.

## Be Flexible

Flexibility is a key characteristic of new businesses, and this extends to the revenue model. Your entire business structure may not change, but the founder must constantly be looking at whether the revenue model is working for the business or not, and if not, what the necessary adjustments are. Hence, an entrepreneur needs to spend a great deal of time forecasting and re-forecasting and looking at which permutation of the revenue model will support his business in the most lucrative way.

Your business hinges on a lot of variables, and it is essential to know how these variables impact the bottom-line, and what factors have the most effect on these variables. Variables are dependent on a number of considerations such as your processes and life cycle. Each variable must be looked at separately, and one way to do this is through a sensitivity graph, which is one that will show where the revenue improves or worsens when manipulating the variables.

It would be silly to have your head in the sand about your variables and their possible impact on your business. They are a risk, and being aware of risk is key to having a successful business. Hence, as an entrepreneur, your aim should be to mitigate the variables. Mitigating variables lends a degree of transparency to your business. This transparency is not just important for you as a business owner, but is also of great interest to your investors.

**Types of Revenue Streams**

Revenue streams can be divided into two categories:

- **Transaction Revenue**: These revenues are earned from the customer making a one-time payment for the product or the rendering of a service.
- **Recurring Revenue:** The recurring revenues are earned from consistent ongoing payments rendered to the company for either the delivery of the value proposition or after sales care for the customer.

# How do companies generate revenue streams?

- **Asset sale:** This kind of sale refers to the transfer of ownership rights of a physical product from the seller to the buyer. At amazon.com, ownership rights of a myriad of products such as books, music and electronics are sold to the buyers. Similarly, Honda sells the ownership rights of the cars it manufactures to buyers, after which the buyer has complete freedom to rent out, use, or even total the car.

- **Usage fee:** This kind of fee is usually charged by service providers to customers for the use of the service. Hence, an internet provider will probably charge a customer for using their line for a certain number of minutes during the day or month. A beautician may charge a customer according to the number and nature of treatments the customer receives.

- **Subscription fees:** When a user requires long-term or continuous access to the products of a company, they pay a subscription fee. Hence, a gym may sell a yearly membership subscription to its customers. Cable providers may charge a subscription fee to its users for which they will pay up front.

- **Lending/ renting/ leasing:** Some organizations provide their customers with exclusive rights to their product for a limited amount of time for a set fee. At the end of this period, the organization regains ownership of the product. This kind of revenue model presents a number of advantages, both for the company and the customer. The company enjoys recurring revenue from the customer for the mentioned period. On the other end of the coin, the customer has exclusive access to the product for the time she requires it without having to make a hefty investment. Hence, zipcar.com a popular car renting service in North America allows customers to rent their cars for a specified time period. This has become a very popular service in the cities in which it is available because it provides customers with the advantage of a car without their having to invest in buying one.

- **Licensing:** Licensing is generally useful for products, services, or ideas that fall under the category of intellectual property. This opens up a revenue stream for rights holders, who would otherwise have had to invest in manufacturing as well. It is common in the technology industry for patent holders to license the use of patents to other companies and to charge a licensing fee for it.

- **Brokerage fee:** When a company acts as an intermediary to ease the communication and transaction between two or more parties, they charge a brokerage fee. An example of this is when a headhunting firm matches a candidate to an organization looking for a particular skill set. The firm usually charges a percentage of the gross salary from the organization, the candidate, or both.

- **Advertising:** Companies that earn a fee through promoting another organization, product, or service charge an advertising fee for their service. Traditionally this kind of revenue was common only in the advertising industry. Recently however, with the boom of the internet and e-commerce, many websites are also using this as a main revenue stream.

## Key Revenue Model Questions

- What benefits are customers currently paying for?
- Are there unrealized benefits that customers would pay more for?
- How are customers paying for these benefits today?
- What type and frequency of payment would be preferable to the status quo?
- What percentage of the total revenue does each revenue stream represent?

# Case Study: Google's Revenue Model

As you may know, many of Google's services are provided for free for the individual user. A significant portion of Google's revenues are derived from advertising that companies pay to reach users online. Google helps advertisers create advertisements through its auction-based program, Google Adwords. Advertisers then pay Google based on customer clicks on the advertisements available. Google also provides advertisers with to its network members through its Google Adsense program. Another option available to advertisers is Google's DoubleClick technology through which audio and video advertisements are made available on Google Network member sites.

Google has generated ninety-six percent of its revenues from advertising for the past several years as opposed to Apple, that has earned seventy percent of its revenues through the sale of its products. Google has been experimenting with other possible revenue streams by evolving its search offerings, extending into mobile, and trying its hand at a Google-based operating system. It has even expanded into enterprise-based solutions.

# 5.2 COST MODEL

In this chapter, we will examine the cost structure of a startup, the types of cost structures, characteristics of cost structures, and a brief case study of cost structures. This will enable you to evaluate the cost of creating and delivering the value proposition and of creating and sustaining your revenue streams.

When creating your cost model, it is imperative to ask the following questions:

- What activities create costs in your startup?
- Are these activities matched to the Value Propositions for your startup?
- Is your startup more value-driven or cost-driven?

# What are the types of businesses based on cost structure?

Cost is a common concern for all businesses. Select businesses make it their mission to minimize costs as much as possible, and all of their strategies and tactics are derived from this goal. Businesses can be categorized into two extremes: cost driven or value driven. Realistically, companies often sit in the middle of this spectrum.

### Cost-driven businesses

This model is focused on reducing costs. A business which is cost driven focuses on creating a lean cost structure by offering low-priced value propositions, a high degree of automation, and outsourcing of costly functions. It is important to lower your prices based on internal costs and expenses rather than in response to what the competition is doing. Industries prone to price wars experience this tragedy all the time. During the price war, competitors will steadily undercut each other's prices to attract the price-sensitive customer. However, if your competition is able to manage its costs and create operational efficiencies, they will be able to sustain its business on the lower price and continue to attract customers. If your business fails to do so, you may end up arriving at a price you are stuck with that is untenable, an unrealistic situation considering your expenses.

### Value-driven businesses

Not all companies are driven by cost. Some focus completely on the value they are providing to their customers, taking the value-driven approach. This strategy is characterized by complete focus on the creation and delivery of a high-value value proposition that is highly customized to the customer segment's preferences. Luxury hotels opt for a value-driven approach. The Hyatt prides itself on its customer service and amenities. They put a lot of effort into creating an experience for which customers are willing to pay top dollar. Employees of the hotel are encouraged to anticipate individual customer's needs, down to greeting a repeat customer by name and providing her with a room with her preferences already in place.

# What are the characteristics of cost structures?

Cost structures have multiple characteristics, as discussed earlier. These are highlighted below:

## Fixed Costs

Fixed costs are business expenses that remain the same regardless of the volume produced by the business. These costs such as monthly salaries or rent for office space are usually time bound and can also be referred to as overhead costs. Manufacturing businesses are typically characterized by high fixed costs caused by the investment required in renting the facilities and the equipment. However, it is important to note that fixed costs will not remain the same forever. Instead, they may change with time, but will remain stable over a period of time. Hence, these costs are also known as sunk costs for the relevant period of time.

## Variable Costs

Variable costs are costs which are heavily dependent on the volume of output a company produces. These are costs incurred when you produce a product. If you do not produce, you will have no variable costs. Similarly, you may have delivery costs, but if customers aren't asking for delivery, then this is possibly a variable cost that you can avoid. These costs are therefore sensitive to changes in demand and supply and cannot be easily predicted. They increase in direct proportional to increases in labor and capital. Examples of variable costs include utility bills and raw materials used for production of the end product. The organization and execution of a music festival will typically be characterized by high variable costs.

Another cost close to the management's hearts and minds are operational costs or OPEX. These are the costs associated with the day-to-day running of the company, the used-up expenses. A 3D printer may be an example of an expense that falls in OPEX. Other OPEX-related expenditures include the purchase of raw materials, electricity bills, and expenditure on maintenance of buildings and machinery.

**Economies of Scale**

Economies of scale exists when a higher production volume results in a lower total cost-per-unit for production. Economies of scale are a benefit enjoyed by many large companies with a high production levels. This is a cost advantage which big companies can enjoy due to their size, quantity of production, and scale of operations. The reason costs fall with higher volumes is because higher volumes spread fixed costs more thinly, making the cost-per-unit fall dramatically; thus, the average cost per unit is reduced. A large company will often have a lower cost-per-unit output than a smaller company; a company with more facilities will have more of an advantage than one with fewer facilities. Not only do economies of scale help lower fixed costs, they may also help reduce variable costs by creating synergies and increasing efficiency.

Bulk buying is a common indicator of mass production and automatically leads to economies of scale. Bulk buying often leads to lower prices. When you are buying in volume, you often have a stronger negotiating position and can create lower prices for your raw material. This is a tactic used most successfully by Walmart, which uses bulk buying to negotiate much lower prices for the items in its stores. It is then able to transfer these savings to its customers, providing them with lower than market prices for regular items.

## Economies of Scope

Economies of scope refer to the reduction of costs when a business invests in multiple markets or a larger scope of operations. The average cost of production generally decreases if a company opts to increase the number of goods it produces. A company will have a structure in place already, along with all of the requisite departments such as Marketing, Finance, and Human Resources; therefore, the company can increase their scope and economize the entire structure.

Economies of scope based on product diversification are only achieved if the different products have common processes or share the use of some of the resources. Spending on marketing the products or distribution channels may lessen per unit if both products require similar marketing efforts or use the same distribution channel.

Economies of scale can be easy to achieve and measure: the use of product bundling and family branding are examples of firms trying to achieve economies of scale. However, economies of scope present a bigger challenge in terms of measurement. Still, economies of scope have multiple advantages for the business, including:

- A great deal of flexibility in the design and mix of the product,
- Increased response rate and decreased response time to market-driven changes,
- Repeatable processes with a higher degree of control over their execution,
- Reduced costs through minimizing waste,
- More accurate predictions of changes and cycles,
- More efficient use of hardware and software, and
- Less risk.

## Case Study of Google's Cost Structure

Google's cost elements can be divided into four categories:

- Research and Development (R&D),
- Data Center Operations,
- Traffic Acquisition, and
- Sales and Marketing.

Google invests deeply into its R&D to develop improvements of existing products and constantly create new and innovative solutions. This expenditure has helped Google maintain its position at the top, despite the typical short-lived cycles of popularity of most Internet-based successes. This has led to economies of scope for Google and has resulted in a great deal of product diversification, examples of which include Google's entry into the mobile app market as well as its cloud-sharing services.

It is speculated that Google has almost a million servers globally and that these servers help process around a billion search requests daily. Google has invested a great deal into these data centers, and they represent a significant fixed cost for the company. Even the management of these servers represents a major cost for the company. However, due to the high volume of searches these centers process, they are able to increase economies of scale for the company by optimizing the servers' search capacities.

Traffic acquisition costs refer to the money given to the Google Network through its Adsense program or to websites which redirect users to Google or provide the Google Toolbar to their customers. All of these players help Google to attract more and more users to its products and services daily.

Finally, Google invests in advertising and marketing to the wide customer base it is targeting. These costs also include the worldwide sales force that Google maintains, a group which aims to sell its campaigns as well as its support team that is available to handle customer complaints or concerns.

# 5.3 SALES MODEL

In this chapter, we introduce the sales process, describe the steps of the sales process, and discuss how to improve the sales process.

The sales process is a term that is used to refer to the method or approach of selling a product or a service to the customers. This process includes the plan for selling, as well as the interactions between the buyers, the salespersons, and the company. The sales process is a structured approach that starts with identifying prospective customers and ends with delivering the product.

Sales is one of the most important determinants of the likelihood for profits and profitability. This is why it is important to have a standardized and well-planned process to make sales. It is valuable to plan and monitor the interactions with prospective customers from the first communication to the last step of closing the deal. The entire process involves efforts and engagement of not just salespersons, but also strategy makers, decision makers, and other members of the sales department.

# The Eight Steps of the Sales Process

The sales process is a step-by-step procedure that eventually leads to completing the sale, and it is generally divided into eight main steps that many businesses follow. The main benefit of dividing the process into these steps is that doing so results in easy execution and understanding, as well as division of responsibilities among various sales professionals. Also, by dividing the process into parts, one small goal can be achieved at a time, making the overall process easier.

## Step #1: Prospecting

Prospecting is the first and one of the most important steps or parts of the sales process. Prospecting basically involves looking for new prospects or potential buyers, and the key to this step is knowing where to look. One way in which this can be done is by making a list of the existing customers and then figuring out the best strategies of approach for each category of customer. It is important that you know what the differences are between leads, qualified prospects, and prospects. Make sure you don't waste your time in searching out those who may not give in or buy.

## Step #2: Pre-approach – Planning of the sale

Now that you have searched for prospects or possible buyers, it is time to plan the method to approach these prospects with a deal or sales pitch in which they might interested. This is an important step, as it involves your first interaction or communication with your possible long-term customers, and you do not want to make mistakes here. It is the beginning of a new association or relationship, and there must be a proper plan or strategy of approach. Planning is a process that can sometimes take time, high-level expertise. and experience from established sales experts.

## Step #3: Cross questioning and identification

The next step in the sales process is to find out what the needs of your prospects are. Without knowing or analyzing their needs, you may not be able to provide them with the product or service they are looking for. Identification of what the requirements of the customer base is usually involves asking questions, noting answers, and then evaluating those answers to come up with customized solutions. From here, you may be able to qualify your prospects so that you know whether you should pursue them further or not.

## Step #4: Assessing the needs

Once the identification of those potential buyers who are suitable for your product type has been accomplished, the next step is to analyze and assess their needs and what their expectations are from the products that you are offering. Needs assessments can best be accomplished via prospective customer face-to-face interview or through video conference. This step helps to identify the main requirements of most prospective clients so that efforts can be made to fulfill those needs.

## Step #5: Presenting the sales pitch

The focus of a business or seller must be to focus on the benefits of the product or service to the customers, rather than focusing on features. This will help the business to create a presentation that highlights the benefits of the product to the customers rather than putting stress on the features possessed. This step involves the creation of an excellent sales presentation that takes the perspective of the customers rather than the business. The previous step of needs assessment must be fully incorporated within this step to engage and intrigue the audience.

## Step #6: Addressing concerns

When you go on the path of the sales process, then you will interact and communicate with prospective buyers, and this will let you know about customer objections, concerns, and grievances. As a seller who is trying to satisfy consumers in the best possible way, it becomes your responsibility to address these concerns and offer a solution accordingly. The product or service thus offered must be free of any problems that might bother the customer. Doing so will not only improve the trust that your prospects place in you, but will encourage them to buy from you immediately.

## Step #7: Closing the sales

Closing is the process of furthering the sales process and finalizing the deal. This is the step when the prospect agrees to purchase the product or service or makes the payment. This is the part of the sales process when all obstacles have been overcome, and results finally begin to show themselves. Closing may, however, mean different things in different scenarios and parts of the sales process. For example, closing might occur when a salesperson manages to get an appointment, or it might occur when the customer asks 'what is the price' and so on.

## Step #8: Following up

One of the most neglected, yet important parts of the sales process is the part that follows the close, and it is called follow-up. When a salesperson has managed to close the sale, that person should follow up with the prospect or customer in order to nurture the relationship further with the aim of not letting the prospect change his mind. This is a good way to remain in the mind of the prospect and may even require some persistence. This is a way to ensure that those whom you have already converted continue shopping from you and those who haven't are given more reasons to convert.

# How to Improve the Sales Process

The growth of a startup is not merely dependent upon the amount of profits that it makes, but also on the kind of customer experience it provides and the way the sales process is handled. A well-planned sales process cannot be considered equivalent to a good sales process. Most businesses work on a static sales and business model that stops working after a point, or shows results only to a limited extent. In such a scenario, in order to improve sales and the way you serve your consumers, it is important to work upon refining and improving each step of the entire sales process. Working on the customer experience at each of the touch points is the key to better performance and long-term benefits. The following are some of the main ways to work on the sales performance at each of the steps:

**At Step #1 (Prospecting)**

Do you know that it is typically harder to acquire a new customer than to sell to an existing one? If the first step of finding and acquiring new prospective buyers can be improved, selling products can be made easier. There are many ways to improve upon the process at the step of prospecting. One of the first ways is to improve the referral system with existing customers. The better the referral system, the easier will it be to find potential customers. By making a list of the existing customers and dividing customers into groups on the basis of the approach needed to connect to them, you will be able to explore the various ways there are to acquire prospects. This is not just a one-time effort or activity. The more potential buyers you can identify, the greater the opportunity for sales.

## At Step #2 (Planning the Sale)

Once you have developed a list of prospective customers, the next step is to work on the method of contacting them. This is the step in which you make the first contact with your prospective customers, and it must be impressive and convincing. If not, you may lose a valuable prospect. At this stage, the guard of prospective customers is up, and to bring it down, you will need to present yourself and your company in such a way that the prospect feels like you really have something great to offer. One way to make the first contact is by making a highly effective and well-scripted sales call. If the needs of the customers are focused on more than the features of your service, then your chances of success will be higher.

## At Step #3 (Cross-questioning and Identification)

Once you have contacted all of you prospective customers, you may develop an understanding of which prospects are unlikely to buy. The term for identifying the most likely customers and removing the less likely ones is "identification." To improve the identification step, ask key questions of the prospects. Make sure you prepare a list of all possible questions that can help with this step. Sample questions include:

- **Are they the decision makers?** The first thing that you must know is whether the person you are dealing with is the one who will make the ultimate buying decision or if others are involved.
- **Do they have similar products?** Another thing that you must know is whether your prospect owns a product of the same category.
- **Is your product better than the others?** If the product being offered by you is no better than the one already owned, then the prospect is unlikely to buy from you. It is not advisable to waste your time and theirs by advancing further.

**At Step #4 (Assessing the Needs)**

A needs assessment enables you to know how you can be of use or service to the prospect. It is the responsibility of each salesperson to assess or evaluate the needs, requirements, and expectations of the potential buyers in order to deliver the solution closest to their needs. The only way to know this is by asking several intelligently framed, well-planned questions. Asking these questions not only helps you to know what your customers want, but also makes them feel that you genuinely care about them and thereby gain their trust. These answers also enable you to figure out what issues that the prospect has. The questions must be put forth politely and in a conversational tone; the questions shouldn't sound overbearing.

**At Step #5 (Presenting the Sales Pitch)**

Making a presentation is the next step of the sales process, and it requires a lot of pre-planning and brainstorming. In order to improve upon your presentation, follow these steps:

- **Do your research.** It is important to know the audience beforehand so that the presentation can be tailor made for them. This requires you to do research beforehand. A well-prepared and well-researched presentation will not only help gain trust, but also impresses the audience.

- **Work on your look.** The presentation cannot be made casually, and it is important that you look both professional and serious.

- **Have a conversational tone.** It is true that a presentation is usually not a two-way street, but it is crucial that you have a conversational tone and engage your audiences as much as possible. This helps to build rapport and keeps the prospect interested.

- **Set a time limit.** It is important to set a time limit and not go beyond that time in your presentation. It must not be too long, as lengthy ones tend to get boring.

## At Step #6 (Addressing Concerns)

If you think that objections are problematic, then you probably aren't seeing the whole picture. It is important to know and address the objections and concerns of the prospects, as concerns are actually a good sign that they are interested in buying from you. In this step, it is important to:

- **Listen patiently.** The first tip to address concerns is to listen patiently to the objections of the prospects. Give the prospects a chance to explain themselves.
- **Show concern.** The prospect will know that you truly care if you show some concern and briefly repeat what they have said. This shows that you have been listening intently and will genuinely consider action.
- **Check back with a solution.** Offer the prospect a solution during this meeting or reconnect at a later date with a solution.
- **Get back to the conversation**. After concerns have been addressed, make it a point to get back to the conversion and move again to the sales process.

## At Step #7 (Closing)

Closing is an essential part of the sales process, one that is vital to generating sales and profits. The first step to improving this step is to make sure you that you actually do it. The next is to ensure that you get a definite answer before pausing or breaking communication with the prospect. Broadly speaking, closing is a lot about finding out the obstacles and overcoming them. There are many ways in which you can close, but to improve the process, take into account these considerations:

- If the prospect shows any negative signs, aim to convert the negative into a positive and set up a date for the next appointment.
- If the customer asks for the price of the product or service, make advancements in the process and quickly close the deal.

## At Step #8 (Following Up)

Following up can sometimes become a process such that the salesperson becomes bothersome or too persistent. Make sure you stay on the forefront of the prospect's mind, but in a subtle way. Following up should never really end, even if the pace slows over time. Ways to follow up include promotional messages, emails, and phone calls. This helps to gauge the willingness of the prospects to buy from you or to continue the conversation or communication from the point where it was last left.

# 5.4 FUNDING MODEL

We can explore how startups typically raise money by examining how a hypothetical startup would secure its initial funding.

## 1.  Idea Stage

At first it is just you: you are the one with the idea. The moment you started working, you started creating value for the startup. That value will later translate into equity (the percentage of the ownership of the startup), but since you own one hundred percent of it now and since you are the only person in your still-unregistered company, you are not even thinking about equity yet.

## 2.  Co-Founder Stage

As you start to explore the idea and its commercialization potential, you realize that it is taking you longer to make progress than initially expected. You know that you could really use another person's skills. Thus, you look for a co-founder. You find someone who is both enthusiastic and smart. You work together for a short time on your idea, and you see that she is adding a lot of value. You offer her a position as co-founder. You can't pay her any money (and if you could, she would become an employee, not a co-founder), so you offer equity in exchange for work (also known as sweat equity). How much equity should you offer? Ten percent? Twenty-five percent? After all, it is your idea. But then you realize that your startup is worth practically nothing at this point since there are no customers or even a real product, and your co-founder is risking her time as well. You decide that since she will do half of the work, she should receive the same as you, fifty percent. Otherwise, she might be less motivated than you. A true partnership is based on respect. Respect is based on fairness. Anything less than fairness will fall apart eventually. And you want this venture to last. You give your co-founder fifty percent of the startup.

## 3. The Family and Friends Round

You think of placing an advertisement online saying, "Startup investment opportunity." But your lawyer friend tells you that would violate securities laws. As a private company, asking for money from the public is public solicitation, an illegal action for private companies such as yours. So whom can you take money from?

- **Accredited Investors.** Accredited investors are people who either have $1 million in liquid assets or make $200,000 annually. They are the "sophisticated investors," that is people who the government thinks are smart enough to decide whether to invest in a high-risk investment like a startup. What if you don't know anyone with $1 million? You are in luck, because there is an exception that allows startups to raise funding from people who are not accredited investors. These are friends and family.

- **Friends and Family.** Even if your friends and family are not as rich as an accredited investor, you can still accept their money in exchange for equity in your startup. That is what you decide to do, since your co-founder's aunt is interested. You give her five percent of your startup in exchange for $15,000. Now you can afford to build your prototype.

- **Registering the Company.** To give the aunt the five percent you registered the company, either through an online service like LegalZoom or through a lawyer. You issued common stock, gave five percent to the aunt, and set aside twenty percent for your future employees as the "option pool."

## 4. The Angel Round

With the aunt's cash in hand and six months before it runs out, you realize that you need to start looking for your next funding source right now. If you run out of money, your startup dies. So you look at the options:

- **Accelerators and Incubators.** These programs often provide money, office space, and advisors. A typical level of funding is $25,000 for six percent of the startup.
- **Angel Investors.** An average angel round may be $100,000 to $500,000. Angels may focus on startups that they value at $2.5 million or more. Now you have to ask if you are worth $2.5 million today. How do you know? It's a negotiation with the angel investors. Let's say it is still early days for you, and your working prototype is not that far along. You find an angel who looks at what you have and thinks that it is worth $1 million. They may agree to invest $200,000.

Now let's count what percentage of the company you will give to the angel. Not twenty percent. We have to add the 'pre-money valuation', which is how much your startup is worth before new money comes in, and the investment.

$$\$1,000,000 + \$200,000 = \$1,200,000 \text{ post-money valuation}$$

First you take the money, then you give the shares of equity. If you gave the shares before you added the angel's investment, you would be dividing what was there before the angel joined.

Now divide the investment by the post-money valuation $\$200,000/\$1,200,000 = 1/6 = 16.7\%$
The angel gets 16.7% of the startup, or one sixth.

What about you, your co-founder, and her aunt? How much do you have left? All of your stakes will be diluted by one sixth.

Is dilution bad? No and yes. No, because the value of your startup company is growing larger with each investment. But also yes, dilution is bad, because you are losing a level of control of your startup. What should you do? Take investment only when it is necessary. Only take money from people you respect.

## 5. Venture Capital Round

Finally, you have built your first version product, started selling, and you have traction with customers. You approach the venture capitalists (VCs). How much money can VCs invest in you? They typically invest at least $500,000, and often over $1,000,000 in a first round. Let's say the VC values your startup at $4 million. Again, that is your pre-money valuation. She says she wants to invest $2 Million. The math is the same as in the angel round. If you agree to this valuation and the amount of money invested, the VC gets 33.3% of your startup.

Your first VC round is your series A. If you raise additional money from VCs in the coming months or years, these are referred to as series B, C, etc. Eventually, most startups either run out of funding and reach a point in which no one will want to invest, and the startup closes. Or you secure enough funding to build grow your startup to a size where another company wants to buy you, and they acquire you. Or you do so well that you are able to take the startup public through an initial public offering (IPO).

## 6. IPO

Why do companies go public? There are two basic reasons. Technically, an IPO is just another way to raise money, but this time from millions of regular people that buy stock in Apple, IBM, Netflix, and other publicly traded companies. Through an IPO, a company can sell stock on the stock market, and anyone can buy the stock. Since anyone can buy, you can likely sell a lot of stock right away, rather than go to individual investors and ask them to invest. This can be an effective and efficient way to raise a significant amount of funding for your company.

There is another reason to IPO. All those people who have invested in your company so far, including you, are holding "restricted stock." This is stock that you can't simply sell for cash. Why? Because this is stock of a company that has not been verified by the government, which is what the IPO process does. Unless the government sees your IPO paperwork, you may be a fraud, for all people know. The government thinks it is not safe to let regular people invest in such companies, hence the laws related to accredited investors and fundraising. The people who have invested so far in your startup typically desire to convert or sell their restricted stock for cash or unrestricted stock, which is easily sellable. A liquidity event is when what you have in restricted stock becomes easily convertible into cash.

There is another group of people who really want you to IPO: investment bankers like Goldman Sachs and Morgan Stanley. They will give you a call and ask to be your lead underwriter, which is the bank that prepares your IPO paperwork and will connect with their wealthy clients to sell them your stock. Why are the bankers so eager? Because they earn approximately seven percent of all the money you raise in the IPO. If your startup raised $235,000,000 in the IPO , seven percent of that is about $16.5 million for the investment bankers.

Last but not least, a number of your "sweat equity" investors were the early employees who took stock in exchange for working at lower salaries and living with the risk that your startup might fold. The IPO is an opportunity for them, and the founders, to reap significant rewards for their contributions to your startup.

# Worksheet for

# The Startup Analysis Canvas Project
# Phase 4 – Financial Strategy

Each of the phases build on one another as they're all connected to the same new product or service idea. In this phase, you will craft the Financial Strategy for your new startup.

## 1. Revenue

- What types of revenue streams are used by your leading competitors?
- What types of revenue streams will your startup company use and why?
- What are the estimated revenues in year one and year two for your startup company?
  - Justify your estimates using your previously developed market analysis and pricing strategy.

## 2. Cost

- What activities create costs in your startup company?
  - Itemize these costs for year one and year two.
- Are these activities matched to the value propositions for your company?
  - Describe why.
- Is your company more value-driven or cost-driven?
  - Describe why this is appropriate for your target market.
- Do economies of scale and/or economies of scope impact your company?
  - Describe why or why not.

## 3. Sales

- What is the sales process for your leading competitors?
- What sales process will your startup company use?
    - o  Describe why this is appropriate for your target market.

## 4. Funding

- What startup costs are necessary for your startup company?
    - o  Itemize these costs and explain your rationale.
- What are your total estimated expenses before you would be operating at a break-even point?
- What sources of funding are most appropriate to cover these expenses?

# 6.0 NEXT STEPS

Now you are ready to apply The Startup Analysis Canvas to help you:

**Understand** the theory and practice of value creation,

**Determine** how to build the right team for your startup company,

**Avoid** wasting time with startup ideas with limited commercial potential, and

**Raise** the right financial capital at the right time for the right purpose.

You are well positioned to:

**Design value propositions** that directly align with your target customers' interests,

**Assemble and lead a well-comprised team** to produce results that create value for your customers,

**Pursue big ideas** that really matter to customers, and

**Craft a financial model** that minimizes risks and maximizing your success.

You are ready to create your **value proposition**, **team strategy**, **market strategy**, and **financial strategy**. If you have a product or service idea, this makes building a startup visible and tangible, and thus easier to design and manage. If you do not yet have that big idea, I encourage you to read The Opportunity Analysis Canvas, the precursor to this book. Together, they form the foundation of a suite of startup creation tools.

## The Startup Analysis Canvas

| 1 Value Proposition | Problem | 2 Team Strategy | Founders |
|---|---|---|---|
| | Competition | | Advisers |
| | Product-Market Fit | | Partners |

| 3 Market Strategy | Price | 4 Financial Strategy | Revenue Model |
|---|---|---|---|
| | Placement | | Cost Model |
| | Promotion | | Sales Model |
| | | | Funding Model |

# Worksheet for

# The Startup Analysis Canvas Project

# Phase 5 – Final

In this final phase, your challenge is to integrate and enhance your prior four analyses to develop a comprehensive, research-based analysis of your startup company.

## 1. The Problem

- What is the problem?
- What evidence supports that the problem exists?
- Is the problem urgent, underserved, unworkable, and/or unavoidable?
- Is the problem conspicuous and/or critical?

## 2. The Customer

- Who is the target customer?
- What are their needs and wants?
- What is the market size?

## 3. The Value Proposition

- What gains will customers experience?
- What pains will customers experience?

## 4. The Minimum Viable Prototype

- Who are the competitors and their customers?
- What are our minimum viable features?
- Why are these features valuable and rare?
- What is our prototype?

## 5. The Price

- What are the competitors' pricing strategies and prices?
- What are our pricing strategy and prices?

## 6. The Placement Strategy

- What are our distribution channels?
- Who are our intermediaries?

## 7. The Promotional Strategy

- What is the advertising plan and budget?
- What is the public relations plan?
- What is the personal selling plan?
- What is the direct marketing plan and budget?
- What is the sales promotion plan and budget?

## 8. The Sales Process

- What is our sale process?

## 9. The Revenues and Costs

- What are our itemized estimated costs in year one and year two?
- What types of revenue streams are used by competitors?
- What types of revenue streams will we use?
- What are our estimated revenues in year one and year two?

## 10. The Funding Plan

- What are our funding requirements?
- Who are our candidate sources of funding?

## 11. The Team

- Who are the founders?
- Who are the advisors?
- Who are the key partners?

33052708R00133

Made in the USA
Middletown, DE
10 January 2019